# COMING OF AGE
# IN THE RUSSIAN REVOLUTION

# COMING OF AGE IN THE RUSSIAN REVOLUTION

## The Soviet Union at War, Volume 4

### Elena Skrjabina

*Foreword by Harrison E. Salisbury*

*Translated, Edited, and with an Introduction by*

## Norman Luxenburg

Transaction Books
New Brunswick (U.S.A.) and Oxford (U.K.)

Library of Congress Catalog Number: 85-4718
ISBN: 0-88738-034-4 (cloth)
Printed in the United States of America

**Library of Congress Cataloging in Publication Data**
Skrjabina, Elena, 1906–
    Coming of age in the Russian Revolution.

    The 4th vol. of the author's biography, the 1st vol. of which is entitled
Siege and survival, the 2d, After Leningrad, and the 3d, The Allies on
the Rhine, 1945–1950.
    1. Skrjabina, Elena, 1906–        . 2. Soviet Union—History—Revo-
lution, 1917–1921—Personal narratives. 3. World War, 1939–1945—
Personal narratives, Russian. 4. Russian S.F.S.R.—Biography. I. Lux-
enburg, Norman, 1927–        .II. Title.
DK265.7.S595A33        1985        947.084'0924        [B]        85-4718
ISBN 0-88738-034-4

# Contents

# FOREWORD

## *Harrison E. Salisbury*

Few persons have more poignantly captured the continuing tragedy of the contemporary Russian generation than Elena Skrjabina. First came her classic diary of the Leningrad siege that she endured with her family. She was one of the few family members who managed to survive. Then came her story of her trials and sufferings under German occupation and her good fortune to escape being repatriated to her homeland at the end of World War II. And now comes this evocative memoir of a life that has completely vanished, prerevolutionary Russia and the early almost innocent days of the Bolshevik regime.

Alexei Tolstoy wrote a major Russian novel, *Calvary,* in which he sought to recapture some of the scenes and some of the sufferings Skrjabina endured. But here we have one woman's life in vivid and intimate detail—the sunny days of childhood in Nizhny-Novgorod and St. Petersburg, the threatening years before the outbreak of World War I, and the Revolution and devastation in the countryside in 1917 and 1918.

Skrjabina's father was a right-wing member of the Duma. He was extremely conservative, but he was dedicated to the parliamentary principles that had only a brief half-life in the period between the Russian revolutions of 1905 and 1917. When 1917 came he was quickly swept up into the White movement that was in opposition to the Communists; but the struggle was doomed and within a few years he died in Paris, part of the endless human debris tossed up by Russia's internal convulsions.

Elena Skrjabina went on living under the Soviets. She managed to marry, bear children, find work, and then, after Lenin's death, she watched with almost unbearable anxiety as friends and relatives vanished into the insatiable maw of Stalin's prison apparatus. In the end she was one of the few survivors. The Leningrad siege and famine and the terrible trials of World War II took most of the rest.

Yet, within this context there were sunny moments, little bits of time when it seemed that the terrible tiger of fear had been pushed into the corner and life would again be possible. But never was the fear or the terror absent for long. It came back again and again and was to do so as long as Stalin lived. (Nor did it entirely disappear after his death.) Yet there were decent, human, and friendly Communists who helped Skrjabina and her family alongside the toadies and tale-tellers. In the end it was the party people who seemed to suffer more in the purges than the nonparty nonpoliticals like Skrjabina.

This book is valuable as an addition to the mounting record of what conditions were like in the Soviet Union in the 1920s and 1930s. It is a record that has tended to become a bit diffuse with the natural attention in recent years to the dissident movement and the manner of life within the Soviet Union in the post-Stalin and post-Khrushchev period.

Skrjabina saw life from a little corner. She was not at the center of events. She once met Premier Aleksei Kosygin before the war when he was a vigorous young man on the way up, but she was too apolitical to understand that he was a coming man. (And in fact, Kosygin was almost to suffer extinguishment at the hands of Stalin before he finally emerged after Khrushchev as a pillar of the regime.)

Skrjabina's four books, in effect, tell the story of her life up to its happy outcome, an academic career in the United States and years of pleasant teaching at the University of Iowa. Her works are a monument to those qualities of fortitude and survival without which the Russian people would not have been able to endure the terrible hardships imposed upon them by an unbroken succession of tyrannical rulers.

# INTRODUCTION

*Norman Luxenburg*

In 1912 Professor Skrjabina's father, Alexander Gorstkin, was preparing to move his family to the then Russian capital of St. Petersburg, currently Leningrad, in order to take his seat in the Russian parliament (the Duma). The St. Petersburg into which young Elena was moving in 1912, on the eve of the 300th anniversary of the beginning of the Romanov dynasty on the Russian throne, was a very cosmopolitan modern city. It had been growing enormously, from 485,000 inhabitants in 1850 to 1.1 million in 1880, to over 2 million in 1912. Streetcars, plumbing, electricity, and telephones had come to the capital. In 1912, St. Petersburg had more telephones per capita than had Paris. Although there was certainly considerable poverty in Russia, Elena was insulated from the problems of "peasant Russia," the Russia of the bulk of the population.

This St. Petersburg of 1912 was a fast-growing, fast-changing city, and the Russia of 1912 and the prewar period was a fast-changing country, developing in a multitude of directions. The changes, when looked at dispassionately, were overwhelming.

Only 50 years before 1912 virtually no Russian cities were serviced by railroads. The entire nation had but 1,000 miles of track. By 1912, all major Russian cities were serviced by railroads and the trans-Siberian line linked St. Petersburg, Moscow, and other Russian cities, with Vladivostok and the Pacific, 7,000 miles away. The rail network was increasing rapidly, and by 1912 Russia had more miles of track than any other nation in the world except for the United States. Naturally, the West European rail systems, especially those of England and Germany, were far more developed than those of Russia; however, they had virtually reached their optimum of density and that of Russia was still growing.

Fifty years before 1912 there had been but 400,000 students in all the educational institutions of Russia. By 1895 there were 2.5 million, by

3

1905 5.5 million, and by 1915 9.5 million. Fifty years before 1912, prior to the emancipation of 1861, the average Russian was born into serfdom.

Less than 40 years before 1912, before the great military reforms of the 1870s, the average Russian recruit taken into the army faced a 25-year period of service under harsh discipline. The reforms of the 1870s not only reduced the period of service to six years but improved the conditions in the military tremendously.

Almost simultaneously with the military reforms the judicial reforms of the 1870s brought in trial by jury, more competent judges, more just procedures, and put the Russian judicial system on a sound legal basis.

Russian heavy industrial output was climbing rapidly. In the 25-year period prior to 1913, Russian steel production had increased ninefold and Russia had overtaken France to become the fourth largest steel producer in the world. Naturally, the output per capita was considerably lower, and the standard of living of the average Russian in 1912 was still low compared with that of Western Europe. However, the industrial and economic changes in the Russian Empire were enormous. The industrial development was matched by great cultural and political changes and developments, and this was especially true for the capital.

The cultural life of the capital was vibrant with artists, virtually in every field, who could hold their own with the best of those of Paris, London, and other world centers. In the 20 years preceding World War I the city's cultural life had been enriched by Rimsky-Korsakoff, Tschaikovsky, Stravinsky, Rachmaninoff, Skrjabin, Glazunov, and Koussevitsky. St. Petersburg had four opera houses, each offering a full season. Serge Diaghilev had shown the West the Russian ballet, a ballet unsurpassed anywhere. Russian dancers, singers, and writers, from Nijinsky and Chaliapin to Tolstoy and Gorky, were world-reknowned.

A tremendous gulf still separated the intellectual and educated circles from the great masses of the Russian population. However, a young girl coming to the vibrant, beautiful, exciting capital of the most populous non-Asian nation in the world could scarcely be expected to be aware of the long-standing social problems. Neither could she be expected to understand anything of the parliamentary debates between her father and the fast-rising Socialist leader, Alexander Kerensky.

The very fact that in 1912 Russia had a parliament in which voices and opinions opposed to that of the czar's government could be heard was a tremendous development; for only six years earlier, in 1906, it had not existed. By 1912 the Duma had become an accepted and fixed institution in Russian political life.

By 1914 Russia was involved in World War I, during which Russia mobilized the largest army and suffered greater casualties than any army in history. Of some 15 million men who served, there were about 9 million casualties. The Russian transportation system and the comparatively poorly developed financial and industrial establishments buckled under the strain. Food deliveries to some of the major centers, especially the capital, were interrupted. The Russian Army at the front had suffered several major defeats and was being pushed back in Poland. At home the poorly paid industrial proletariat was finding that rampant inflation was cutting into its already low purchasing power. The role of Rasputin around the throne, both real and imagined, had hurt the prestige of the czarist family among those very elements on which it was relying for its main support. In addition, the nationality policy of the czarist regime had created dissatisfaction among many of the non-Russian peoples of the empire.

Under these circumstances it is surprising not that there was a revolution, but that the empire withstood three years of tremendous fighting before the revolution came.

Elena Skrjabina describes how the tremendous military casualties suffered in World War I hit home, how almost all their family friends were losing sons or relatives at the front. She describes the pillaging of the estates and how the supposed "class enemies" were arrested. Impressions of the famine on the Volga in the post—Civil War period, the tremendous housing shortage, the American Relief Administration, the Leningrad famine in the early 1920s that turned people into beasts, all flash through the pages of these remarkable memoirs.

Skrjabina further describes the living conditions in Leningrad in the 1930s; the six-day work-week with jail sentences for those who were late three times; and the chilling feeling of armed men bursting into the apartment at 2:00 or 3:00 in the morning and the fear of not knowing whether the approaching boots in the corridor were coming for someone in your family.

This is the unadorned story of Russian life told by an observant person who lived it; this is a must for those who wish to understand the background of the current Soviet regime.

# 1

# FROM THE DISTANT PAST

In 1912 my parents, two brothers and I, the youngest, were living in Nizhny-Novgorod, present-day Gorky. My eldest brother, Vasili, was studying in St. Petersburg and staying at my aunt's home. Toward the end of May and the beginning of June, when my brothers were finishing their studies in the Nizhny-Novgorod Gentry Institute, plans were being made for our whole family to go to Obrochnoye, our estate in the Lukoyanov district. Although I was always a bit sad to leave our comfortable house and especially my beloved garden, Obrochnoye, with its huge park and its white porticoed house, represented something alluring and romantic to me.

Early in the spring of that year I accidentally overheard a conversation between my parents which extremely puzzled, confused, and saddened me. My mother was saying that it was necessary to start making arrangements for our move to St. Petersburg. I well remember the kind of impression this made on me, and although children love changes, this seemed extremely unpleasant. I threw myself tearfully into Mother's arms, imploring her not to leave Nizhny and my beloved house and garden. Mother, having quietly listened to my outpourings, answered that Father had been elected to the State Duma and that this was a very important matter which was forcing us to settle in St. Petersburg as of the coming fall. None of her explanations made any impression whatsoever on me. St. Petersburg seemed to be something far away, cold, unknown; Nizhny, however, with the magnificent Volga and its sloped shores, with the walks which Nana and I undertook almost every day, with its cheerful fair, and tobogganing on the icy hill—all this seemed so dear to me that I could hardly envision the possibility of leaving. Besides that, all my friends—girls and boys my age—lived here. Especially happy were our Christmas celebrations, when a huge fir tree would be set up in our living room. We children would wait anxiously in the adjoining room until the doors would open and Peter, our servant, in

6

black frock coat and white gloves would solemnly announce, "If you please." Blinded by the lights of dozens of candles, numerous gold and silver toys, gilded nuts, apples, and candy in multicolored wrappings, we would pour into the room. It seemed to me that all of this was now coming to an end.

This St. Petersburg Duma which demanded the presence of my father completely baffled me. Not having received a fully detailed explanation from my mother, I went to Nana, my trusted confidante in difficult times. Nana already knew about the anticipated changes and, like me, did not welcome them. Grieving with me, she nonetheless calmed me by saying that it would not happen right away, that we could still expect a beautiful and magnificent spring in Nizhny; and we could still take our favorite walks along the slopes and our trips on the Volga. She further reminded me that in early June, when my brothers finished their studies, our family would go to Obrochnoye. And this summer, according to Father's promise, I was to receive a horse and would be taught how to ride. For the time being, my sorrow was forgotten.

That summer of 1912 was full of the most interesting experiences. I was supposed to learn French and, as a result of Mother's advertisement, numerous women of all ages came to our home to be interviewed for the position of French governess. This happened every day during the few weeks prior to our departure for the country, and it was a great entertainment not only for me but also for my brothers. Paul and George jumped up at every bell and, hiding behind the door, looked over the candidates. After the departure of each applicant, they would burst into the living room and give Mother all kinds of advice. The older and less attractive women did not fare too well. Following a week of uninterrupted visits and considerations, the unanimous choice fell on an attractive and charming young girl from Lyons—Yvette Delacroix. My mother was completely satisfied with her recommendations, while my brothers were pleased by her youth and appearance.

On the fifth day of June our entire family, including Vasya who had arrived from St. Petersburg, went to Obrochnoye. The major event of this year was to be the July wedding of Uncle Nikolai, my father's youngest brother, to a twenty-year-old student named Olga. Although I did not then understand why, I nonetheless noticed that Grandmother did not approve of her son's fiancée. Only some time later, overhearing an adult conversation, did I understand that Grandmother detested emancipated women. Olga was very self-assured and, in my eyes, very pretty. She acted rather condescendingly toward those around her and entered into quarrels with everyone, including Grandmother. The subject of their discussions was the position of women in contemporary

Russian society. Olga spoke loudly, sharply, and somewhat nasally, which especially irritated Grandmother. Olga Alekseevna, my grandmother, was of the old school and considered a woman's place to be in the nursery, pantry, and even in the kitchen, and that higher education and all these women's courses were not meant for their minds. It was difficult to argue with her; even her sons avoided the issue.

From overhearing conversations between Nana and the servants I concluded that the wedding might not take place. This made me especially sad since I liked Olga very much. She had brought a completely new spirit into the atmosphere of our old estate. In my opinion, it was not at all bad to bring in something new, especially an educated aunt. Moreover, this was my first contact with a young woman who had interests other than the home; and it made a great impression on me. Later in my life, upon finishing high school at the age of sixteen, I dreamed of entering a technical institute and becoming an engineer. The memory of Olga stayed with me, and she served as my model.

In addition to my personal sympathy toward Olga, the possible cancellation of the wedding disturbed me for another reason. I had earlier seen and heard about wedding celebrations in the country, and the idea of riding to church in troikas decked out with bells and flowers very much appealed to me. Later, the adults would be so busy that we children would be free from constant supervision. What a delightful party it promised to be with all the relatives, friends, and neighbors who would come! What pleasure I anticipated from being with my cousins at such a large dinner!

Fortunately, my fears were not confirmed, and on the 24th of July, my name day, the marriage of Olga and Uncle Nikolai was jubilantly celebrated. I will never forget the tens of troikas, one rivaling the other in beauty and speed, the bedecked coachmen wearing multicolored cloaks belted with red sashes, the elegant crowd of guests, the numerous bouquets of flowers, and the solemn church service. I was particularly impressed by the magnificent dinner and the huge table of hors d' oeuvres that was the main attraction for us children.

The second great event of this summer was my father's gift. A beautiful bay mare, Mousme, was placed completely at my disposal and riding lessons began immediately. Paul, an excellent horseman, was entrusted with my training. At first he put me on a Cossack saddle, considering this less dangerous. But I was soon graduated to a magnificent lady's saddle, smelling of new leather. When the appropriate riding habit was fitted and sewn, and a hat with a veil was bought, my pride knew no bounds. The horse was passive and well trained, so that I soon began to ride around the rather large circle especially set up in the meadow behind the house. Either my brother Paul or the stable boy would accompany me, so that I was never all alone. Guests, usually our nearest relatives, would come almost every holiday to the estate; and Paul would then invite them to our "hippodrome" to demonstrate my success. It always seemed so happy and cheerful in Obrochnoye.

The estate was separated into two parts by a large road. The old section, with its ancient trees, birch paths, and large fruit orchard, belonged to Grandmother. The eighteenth-century house, that had acquired the name "old house," was a wooden structure with a great number of rooms; and although it lacked many conveniences, it nonetheless was very comfortable, full of special sounds and smells. Our house, built in 1906, was called the "new house." It was constructed of white stone with tall white columns across the front. In it there was every type of modern convenience, including two bathrooms (a rare luxury in those times) and a huge terrace with a commanding view. My mother, who loved a beautiful view, had ordered part of the orchard to be chopped down in order that the green meadows and the river might be seen. There were far fewer rooms in this house than in the old house; but, on the other hand, all that was beautiful and comfortable had been included. I especially liked the splendid approach to the house, the asphalt rise along which the guests' troikas would roll as they approached the stately porch.

Grandmother united all those around her. At that time she was a little over seventy years old and could still run around playing games with her grandchildren. She would also play bright waltzes and polkas on the piano, forcing everyone, young and old, to dance to her accompaniment. Everyone adored but feared her. She was strict yet held no grudges. At that time she was raising several young orphan girls, training them to become maids in good homes, as she expressed it. And when it came to disobedience, she gave not a thought about employing corporal punishment. The time I first saw her slap Sima, a dear girl with whom I played every day, I burst into a flood of tears. Grandmother, having quickly calmed down, became embarrassed by my strong reaction. She bustled off to the pantry and returned loaded down with a goodly amount of my favorite sweets for Sima and me. Evidently, she rewarded Sima because she had been punished and me because I showed my sympathy. Sima, who had not shed a tear, tried to comfort me by stuffing sweets into my mouth between my sobs.

The children of both family and friends who were staying at the estate went every morning to the old house to say good morning to Grandmother, promptly at nine o'clock. She was always in the dining room, waiting in an armchair surrounded by baskets of chocolates, nuts, and other goodies, tempting to any child. She passed out everything generously, warning us to wait until after dinner. That, of course, we never did; but we never lost our appetites.

I always had to eat dinner in the new house. After finishing dessert, though, my brothers and I hurried to the old house, where dinner usually began later. In this way, we were able to begin all over again with the first course. At first, Mother was angry and reprimanded us for such behavior. Later, she just waved her hand and we would run to Grandmother's inviting house for our second dinner.

By August the happy summer mood had already begun to fade. My parents were discussing the move to St. Petersburg and the necessity of finding an apartment. But the one last good thing we had to look forward to that year was Father's birthday—the 30th of August. On that day there would be just as many guests as on the 24th of July, when Grandmother celebrated her birthday.

Always before the one final event to anticipate with pleasure was our return to Nizhny-Novgorod. How happy I had been each fall to return to all my friends, to my cozy, bright bedroom. There was a rather narrow, little-traveled sidestreet outside my window, where women walked selling milk, vegetables, and berries. They would call out to their customers in loud, singing voices. In addition to these women, a Tartar "prince," that's how they called the Tartar in Nizhny, often came by, buying secondhand goods. But the main attraction was the organ-grinder with his parrot. I would pull myself up onto the wide window ledge and, at the end of his repertoire, throw him the copper coins Father would give me.

All of that was now gone, and the gray sky and the rolling storm clouds made things seem all the more oppressive. I wanted to cry but felt ashamed in the presence of Yvette. She was standing near me, gaily twittering as we entered this city of St. Petersburg that was so mysterious and unattractive to me. It seemed that even my mother shared Yvette's attitude. Mama had spent her youth in St. Petersburg, and she still retained the happiest memories of that time.

When the train stopped, an excited group of people came to meet us: Father, my three brothers, my aunt (Mother's sister), and her sons and daughter. They were all in the best of spirits and pleased by our arrival. My brothers surrounded me, hugging and kissing me, and interrupting each other to tell me about the interesting things and the wonderful presents Father had awaiting me. Knowing his generosity, I already had a foretaste of the pleasant things to come.

We hired carriages and set off toward Panteleymonovskaya Street, where Father had rented an apartment. Even though it had stopped raining, it was still very gray and gloomy. Thus, although it was little more than a fifteen-minute ride from the Nikolaevsky Station to Panteleymonovskaya Street, it seemed to me as though we were dragging along endlessly. But we eventually stopped before a gray, five-story building. In the lobby there was a tiny elevator that barely held two people; we let our parents ride while we walked up to the fifth floor.

I immediately looked over the eight-room apartment. It had a long, narrow hallway, a kitchen, and two servants' rooms; but it did not make a good impression upon me at all. I was particularly disappointed by my room—long, narrow, and even crooked, in no way to be compared with my bright, spacious room in Nizhny-Novgorod. Scarcely holding back the tears, I started to unwrap the packages that were waiting for me; this somewhat diverted my attention from the unpleasant first impressions.

From that day on a completely new life began both for me and for our whole family. My father, being the head of the nobility of the Lukoyanov district and the leader of the zemstvo in Nizhny-Novgorod, had formerly spent the day at home when not away on a business trip. But here in St. Petersburg he went off to the Duma every day from morning until six o'clock in the evening. He was usually in an agitated state when he returned home and, until he calmed down, was so loud and noisy at dinner that he could be heard throughout the house. At the time I was unable to understand what displeased him so much at his new job. There was nobody to ask about it. My brothers felt that I was too young to understand. I could never quite get up the nerve to ask Mother, and Nana understood no more than I did. It was only several years later that much of what was going on became clear to me. Father, an extreme conservative, came in contact with people in the Duma of different parties who freely stated their opinions. It seemed to my father that this was offensive to the czar, whom he venerated.

At the time this was all a complete mystery to me, and it seemed that St. Petersburg itself was responsible for the distress and changes that had come into our lives. "And why did everybody congratulate him in Nizhny? They should have gone and let us stay home," I advised Nana. She agreed with me completely. Despite all of Yvette's enraptured declarations, life had been a lot better for both of us in Nizhny. Here, even in the magnificent Summer Gardens, with its many pathways, the monument to Krylov, Peter the Great's Summer House, and the marble statues, it seemed less lovely than our hillside and beautiful Volga.

Christmas came upon us almost unnoticed. As in previous years, my parents wanted to give me a tree-trimming party and invite children my age, of whom I already knew many. I received several invitations to parties during the first days of the holidays, so my parents decided to plan for our tree-trimming celebration on the fourth day. They did not rush to buy the tree, being used to the familiar merchants of Nizhny who usually brought one to our house. But here things were different. When we went to the tree market on Christmas Eve, all suitable trees were already gone. We returned empty-handed. My disappointment was unbounded. Mother started calling everybody, hoping that someone could help us out or at least give us some good advice. It was all useless. And only on the second day of Christmas, when I had already lost all hope of our having a Christmas tree, a cousin, a young officer, called and offered to bring a tree on the following day. This tree had been set up by the officers of his regiment at a gathering for the soldiers. He did warn us, though, that at the end of the festivities the soldiers were allowed to grab the candy and crackers off the tree and that after their attack it would look pitiful and worn. There was no need for discussion; we were happy to accept.

I long remembered the moment when several soldiers carried the wretched Christmas tree into our apartment. Many of its branches were broken and the tree was indeed in very sad shape. My brothers comforted me, promising to make every effort to repair the damage. I had little confidence in them and tremblingly awaited that evening when my small guests would gather. But when the appointed hour arrived, and my guests, dozens of children who had awaited the opening of the doors to Father's study, tore into the dining room, everyone stood stock still; I could not believe my eyes, so wonderful was the scene presented to us. Apparently my mother and brothers had gone to great lengths to make that poor, bare tree especially attractive.

After New Year's, at the invitation of the Saburov family, my parents took me to Pavlosk for a few days. Saburov was a superintendent at the palace; he had magnificent horses and carriages at his disposal, and he had two girls my age! We took trips to all the surrounding areas: to Tsarskoye Selo, Pulkovo, and Gatchina. The town itself was a charming little town with palace and park all covered with deep, soft snow. We had fun sliding down the huge ice hills that had been constructed in the park, and we took walks along the shoveled pathways of the grand park. It was here that I first knew the pleasures of winter excursions in groups of troikas that were lined up, one after the other.

That year of 1913 was an important year. Grand festivities were to be held on the occasion of the tricentennial of the House of Romanov; and Father, being a member of the Duma, received an invitation to a ball in the Winter Palace. The entire imperial family was to be present. In the city all sorts of celebrations, lights, and fireworks displays were being prepared. But there was an unpleasant incident that took place during the church services at the Kazan Cathedral on the festive day.

Rodzyanko, president of the Duma, reserved seats for the Duma members in the front rows, not far from the imperial family. When he approached the entrance to the cathedral, the doorman warned him that a peasant in silk shirt and high leather boots had gone up to the front and, paying no attention to the guards, refused to leave. Rodzyanko instantly understood that the undesired guest was Rasputin, whom he hated. Incensed by the man's disobedient behavior, he had Rasputin[1] physically removed from the church.

That incident somewhat marred the festive mood of my parents. It was only in the evening, when we rode in Father's hired carriage among thousands of others and our eyes met with the fairyland visions of the city glowing under the multitude of lights, that the unpleasant impressions caused by the morning's incident in the Kazan Cathedral began to fade away.

Soon after this incident, my parents started their preparations for the ball that was to be held in the spring. My mother ordered a dress of white brocade with roses of silver embroidered on a pale-rose underdress. The material was so beautiful that I could hardly contain myself from delight. Mother also was very pleased, as she prepared for the forthcoming ball. My father gave her a bracelet of multicolored sapphires for this day. Years later in Simbirsk this same bracelet, exchanged for salt, flour, and fat, saved us from the unbelievable famine then raging in the Soviet Union.

### VASYA'S ILLNESS AND DEATH

Everything was going along fine. My brothers were studying; Vasya especially stood out because of his great ability, both in his law studies and in his musical career. He not only played at home but even began to give concerts. Paul, on the other hand, was more diligent and hardworking. George lived at the *lycée* and was only home on holidays.

My parents spoke often about politics, about the czarist family, about Rasputin, and the illness of the young heir. At times, however, Mother, in particular, would dream about the forthcoming ball, where they would see the entire court.

It was in March that Vasya unexpectedly took ill. Our family doctor would come almost every day; and at first he did not find anything serious, saying that it was only the usual flu. The first few days Vasya received visits from many friends and acquaintances. He was very happy and joked a lot, as was his custom. From his room almost uninterrupted laughter could be heard, and I liked to go there and listen to the conversations of the adults until my brothers would put me out. Then, insulted, I would go to my room.

The longer this illness continued, the worse it became. Vasya's face became clouded with a yellow tinge, and his spirits noticeably diminished. Our family doctor became seriously worried and requested that we call a famous professor. I was forbidden to enter the patient's room. Paul stopped going to the university and began spending all his days at Vasya's bed. Guests now became a rare occurrence. Mother was very worried. The old professor came frequently and insisted on a council of several specialists. Vasya's illness turned out to be something entirely unknown to the medical world of St. Petersburg. The doctors told Mother that this was the third case that year. The council could not help and did not come to any conclusions. Vasya was lying in bed, pale, yellow, and morose. The family's mood was falling from day to day.

Meanwhile, spring began to make itself felt in St. Petersburg. The snow had still not disappeared entirely, but the first flower merchants were already beginning to appear on the Nevsky Prospekt. Nana would take me out of the house for long periods; and we would roam for hours along the Neva embankments, admiring the moving ice or drop in to the Summer Garden that had now begun to take on a look of spring. Numerous statues were already freed of their winter coverings— wooden boxes to protect them from ice and snow. The roads were cleaned. Children surrounded the Grandfather Krylov statue and buzzed just like a swarm of bees. The heavy, oppressive atmosphere of our apartment was forgotten here in the lap of nature, transformed by spring. We would be detained for long periods of time on the Liteiny Prospekt. This was especially distinguished by the beautiful display windows, and here I would select Easter presents for myself. I was always captivated by the little eggs made of various precious stones that I, as a rule, would receive every Easter from my parents and relatives. I already had several dozen in my collection. Now I would indicate those that I wanted to receive this year.

One morning at the end of March I woke up in a most happy mood, awakened by the sun's rays penetrating the room. That night I had had especially good dreams and was still under their influence. I did not realize right away that everything in the house was not good, that Vasya was still ill, and that yesterday there had again been a council of doctors. A strange noise in the house caused me to jump up quickly. Nana was not in the room. Frightened, I ran down the corridor and almost collided with people carrying our Vasya on a stretcher. I immediately noticed his thin, yellow face, and his sharpened nose. His smooth hair, combed and shiny black, was falling about in disarray. I felt a strange oppressive feeling. It seemed that Vasya had already died. Behind the stretcher came my parents. That same evening Nana and I were alone in the house; my father and mother did not return. Nana told me that they were remaining in the hospital where Vasya had been taken. George was in the *lycée* and Paul had disappeared for the day. Days dragged by, full of fear.

My father would drop in for short periods of time and would again disappear, now to the Duma, now to the hospital. He was in such a mood that nobody would even think of asking him about anything. The cook continued to prepare dinner, but nobody would sit down at the table. Nana would bring our food into the nursery. Paul was almost never at home, or when he was he would eat in the kitchen. Everything seemed upside down; everything had been knocked out of the accustomed routine. The atmosphere was as though a threatening storm cloud was hanging over the house.

But one sunny morning Nana woke me, saying that Mother had returned home and that I could go wake her at nine o'clock as I used to do. I could scarcely wait for the indicated time, and exactly at nine o'clock I was already sitting by her bed. She was still sleeping a heavy and, for her, unusual sleep. I was struck by how much she had changed during that short period since I had last seen her. There was a fearful similarity between her drawn features and those of the ill Vasya. Opening her eyes and seeing me she said, quietly and without expression, "Vasya is no longer with us; the Lord has taken him to heaven."

I was unable to say one word and could not comprehend what had taken place. Vasya, a twenty-year-old handsome, happy, capable young man whom everybody loved would not be with us any longer and had gone somewhere to the unknown. A minute later I broke out in desperate sobbing. Mother did not cry and looked at me with vacant eyes without even trying to calm me. This was my first genuine and heavy grief.

And now everything that we had awaited with such impatience had gone down the drain. For my parents there could be no talk about the ball in honor of the Romanov celebrations. The spring and the approaching Easter holiday—our greatest holiday of the year—no longer held any joy for us.

After the funeral service in the small chapel near the Tavrichesky garden, the coffin with Vasya's remains was put on a funeral wagon; and the family, accompanied by an entire crowd of students, friends, relatives, and acquaintances, proceeded to the Nikolaevsky (now the October) Station. On that very day the coffin was sent to Obrochnoye, where the family crypt was located, and where my older sister had already been buried for almost twenty years. Vasya lay buried in the crypt for seven years; but in 1920 a drunken horde broke into our Obrochnoye Church, took down the bell, took the icons, and having heard a rumor that the dead in our family crypt were buried wearing their gold and silver jewelry, opened the marble slabs and took everything out of the coffins. Not finding any treasures, and apparently angered, they thrust the corpses into other graves. For some reason these drunken bandits desired to put Vasya's skeleton into the coffin of our recently deceased estate manager. Vasya's skeleton was longer than that old man's coffin. Not caring, they cut off his legs and thrust his remains into the coffin, covering the grave with earth. I was told this ten years later by some Obrochnoye residents who were present at this sacrilege. I never told Mother.

That year I spent the most melancholy Easter of my life, despite all the attempts of my aunt and her children to make me happy. I was impatiently awaiting my parents. Neither spring nor the magnificent weather gave me joy.

With the return of my family, my nana and I were taken home. It was time to get ready to go to the country for the summer. That year was the 25th anniversary of my parents' wedding. Last autumn Vasya had come up with the idea for the four of us to take a picture and present this portrait to my parents on their wedding anniversary. For some reason we had not gathered together to do this before his illness. Now Paul suggested that we go and have the portrait made. None of the efforts of the photographer could get us to present a happy appearance; thus, all three of us photographed with sad faces. When in the summer we gave this portrait to our parents, I could see tears in Mother's eyes. It seems that this was the most unsuccessful gift we had ever given.

At the end of April Mother advertised again, only this time for a German governess. The hiring procedure was now entirely different from what it had been a year ago in Nizhny when everyone had been happy. She chose almost the first young German girl who showed up at our house, a girl named Ingeborg. My brothers were not at all interested, and even I was indifferent. Since the death of Vasya, it was as though a cloud had settled over the family. Almost everyone had become apathetic. We went to Obrochnoye in May. En route I tried to speak with my new governess, but my knowledge of German was extremely weak and there was limited conversation. When we at last arrived home, Paul decided to shine. But instead of saying "Wir sind gekommen" (we have arrived), he said "Wir sind gestorben" (we have died). The German girl, not saying a word, just looked at him blankly. After the happy, witty Yvette, Ingeborg, despite her rather pretty face, seemed unattractive to us because of her cold tone of voice and her characteristic reserve.

Somehow or other life soon resumed its accustomed course. But the former happiness and almost unbounded joy that had distinguished our rural life were gone.

A second sorrow entered my young life. Mother came to the conclusion that I was learning foreign languages poorly because I preferred to chatter with Nana and not the governesses. And the latter were learning Russian instead of being able to motivate me to speak one of the other foreign languages. So it had been with Yvette, and the same thing was now happening with Ingeborg. Mother's decision was a complete catastrophe for me. Nana had to leave our house and return to her parents in Obrochnoye. I was now given over completely to my teacher, with whom good relations were never established.

Nor did my grandmother's and my name days bring any joy. My parents began to quarrel often, and on a number of occasions now I heard Mother predict complete ruin for our family if Father would continue to act as he had been doing and not take immediate steps to save our situation. I considered us wealthy, what with all the fields, forests, farms, estates, cattle, that belonged to us; thus, Mama's agitation was completely incomprehensible to me.

In August a young, handsome fellow came to our house and asked to see Father. I did not hear what they were speaking about, but I did notice that at the end of their conversation the young fellow's face brightened, and he was thanking Father for something or other. After he left, a bad scene unfolded between my parents. Mother, always reserved, was speaking this time with such a raised voice that it seemed she was even shouting; Father, however, always agitated even by trifles, was confused and muttered something to justify his action. Mother would not calm down. I began to listen to their conversation, soon understanding that the whole trouble was about a cow that Father had promised to give the young man. This fellow was from one of the poorest families in our village and wanted to get married. However, he had no money for the purchase of a cow. His intended bride's parents were in no way ready to give their daughter in marriage to a completely impoverished suitor, one who could not even supply her with the most basic needs. The suitor had received an unequivocal refusal. In complete despair, for they had been in love a long time, he decided to take the ultimate step and appeal to the landowner. This ran completely against his grain, for he belonged to the village poor; and these people were fiercely opposed to all capitalists and gentry. However, desperately needing the cow, he ignored his political convictions and came to us. My father was impressed both by his story and by the appearance of this young man and agreed to give him not just a calf but a milk cow from the herd. My father himself prepared to go to the farm the next day to select the one that would be especially pleasing to the future bride.

Thus, Father was in the very best mood after his conversation with Ivan. However, he bumped into Mother, who, on hearing the reason for his excellent humor, immediately started a scene. I don't know what agitated Mother more, the loss of the cow or the fact that it was going into the possession of a "clearly revolutionary" element. In any case, my father got an earful. Nonetheless, he, who was usually conciliatory, turned out this time to be firm as a rock. He said that he had given his word and had no intention of changing his mind. Nothing Mother could say or do could affect this decision.

The next day, taking me with him, Father rode out in his small drozhky while everybody in the house was still asleep. I was flattered by the fact that I was included in this affair, and I took great pleasure from the whole procedure of the selection; not only the bride and groom participated but also the bride's parents, who apparently did not believe up to the last minute the story their future son-in-law told them. What especially elated me were the boisterous expressions of gratitude from the entire family. I also liked the cow, and I was in the very best of spirits when the old father of the bride told me, "There now, my lady, learn something from your father; if you will be good to people, the Lord will send you happiness."

Seven years later, I recalled the words of the Obrochnoye peasant. The revolution had come and gone. At that time my mother and I were living in Simbirsk. There was no word from Father or my older brother, who had joined the White Army. George had been inducted into the Red Army. Things were very difficult for us; Mother was bartering, one after another, those jewels and valuables my generous father had once given her. Through an acquaintance, my schoolmate's father, I had obtained a position as a junior office girl in a finance department. The work consisted of the filing of incoming and outgoing papers. I was paid very poorly; but, nonetheless, what I received enabled us to exist.

Once, at the end of the working day, I was detained for some reason and was hurrying to finish the work left me by the office manager. Suddenly I saw a tall, handsome man approach my desk. He was still young, but by his insignia and bearing I recognized the newly appointed director of the entire finance department. It was said of him that he was a high party functionary and that everyone feared him like fire. He headed directly toward me and asked sharply, "What's your name?" I answered. "Whose daughter are you, Sergei's or Alexander's?" was his second question.

Almost fainting from fear at such an unexpected interrogation, I answered timidly, "Alexander's." Not saying one word more, the new director turned and left. Finishing work, I ran home and told Mother about this event, an incident that normally would have seemed unimportant but under present Soviet conditions threatened to have dire consequences. I told Mother that I was sure I would be fired the next day. At the time, in Simbirsk as in other cities, the Soviets were searching out the "former people;" and the fact that the new director was so well informed about our family, even knowing the name of my father and uncle, did not allow any doubt that my service career was at an end.

The next morning, when I timidly entered our office, the manager of our division called me in and congratulated me on my promotion and appointment to the position of assistant to the executive secretary of our department. This was a significant promotion, considering my age and lack of experience. I could hardly believe my good fortune nor understand how it had occurred. The riddle was soon solved, however. Several days later I encountered a pretty young woman on the street who stopped me, saying, "Don't you recognize me, my lady?" (I had long since become unaccustomed to such a form of address and looked at her with surprise.) "I am Tatiana Grigorieva, Ivan's wife. Do you remember you chose a cow for us when we were getting ready to marry? Now Ivan has been named the director of the regional government finance office." Now I understood to whom I was obliged for my promotion and why. I recalled everything as though it were yesterday: the large cattle yard on the farm in Obrochnoye, the pretty cream-colored cow chosen by the modest, pretty girl and the beaming young man in a white embroidered shirt. I also recalled the words of the old father.

That year we left Obrochnoye before Father's name day and returned to St. Petersburg by the end of August. My brothers had to go to school; and a private teacher had been hired for me, again a German, who came three times a week. The remaining time I studied various subjects with Mother, those subjects essential for passing the entry exam for the girls' institute, where my parents were planning to send me.

A few family acquaintances with children my age joined together and organized private dancing lessons in the large, elegant apartment of Colonel Gladky on Tavrichesky Street. The court ballet master was hired, impressing the parents but not the children. The children did not like this tall, handsome gentleman, who was very strict and angrily ridiculed our awkwardness and mistakes. I personally could not complain about him. He apparently was well-disposed toward me and always chose a good partner for me. My mother, who was able to sew very well, made me a light, charming dress of multicolored chiffon. Thanks to her efforts, I was one of the most elegant girls at the dancing classes.

This time is associated in my memory with my first love. At the classes there were about twenty children between the ages of eight and thirteen. From the first day my attention was drawn to a tall, red-cheeked, well-built boy with luxurious light curls. From his appearance one could have taken him for thirteen. His name was Stepan. The only thing I did not like about him was his name. For some reason, I absolutely wanted his name to be Nikita. This name, connected with the Russian past, seemed to me far more romantic. Stepanovs, however, were everywhere in our village; and here in Petersburg our old janitor was also named Stepan. I became reconciled with this name since I liked its bearer so much. Stepan did not particularly care for these lessons and at the beginning was even absent rather often. Then our ballet master resorted to a few tricks. Catching sight of Stepan in the vestibule (Stepan was always late), our teacher immediately released me from my partner and glided elegantly across the floor, taking me to my hero. It seems we made a good couple and were often applauded. This of course was very pleasing to both Stepan and me. Gradually we began to find more and more pleasure in each other's company. Stepan began to stop missing lessons. But, if for some reason he was not at Gladky's, I did not hide my despondency and as a rule danced worse on those days, provoking snickers from my teacher.

After a two-hour lesson, tea would be served along with very tasty cakes and other sweets from the best St. Petersburg pastry shops. For a long time I remembered the cake with strawberries. There was always a large group that gathered for tea. Besides the children and the adults watching our lessons, there were usually brothers and sisters who were supposed to take home those children whose parents had not come. My brother George always came to pick me up. He had grown a lot these last two years; his facial features resembled Mother's, and she was extraordinarily pretty. George was always elegantly attired in his Lycée dress uniform. At tea he never looked at me at all; he was too busy flirting with the pretty girls. I was just as happy to be near Stepan, who would treat me with my favorite delicacies.

Soon after tea everybody would disperse. From the very next day, I would already be impatiently awaiting the coming dance lesson. These dances in Gladky's house, and my puppy love with Stepan, were the brightest memories of my life in St. Petersburg.

Insofar as our domestic circumstances were concerned, they were far from happy. Everybody still mourned Vasya, and the first anniversary of his death was approaching. Somehow, he had always been able to bring everyone together. Everybody loved him: my parents and brothers, acquaintances, and the servants. Happy, intelligent, he either entertained everyone with interesting stories or, outstanding pianist that he was, he would play the entire evening for their entertainment. Our place had always been happy. Now, however, acquaintances and friends gathered at our home infrequently. George spent Monday to Saturday in the Lycée; and modest Paul, a stutterer, saddened by the death of his beloved brother, could in no way replace him in the circle of Vasya's friends and admirers.

Insofar as the political events in our country were concerned, from the conversations of my parents I understood that everything was far from favorable. My father would come home more and more agitated, giving us the details of the Duma sessions and blasting Kerensky, apparently his bitterest foe. Often the name Rasputin [1] would slip out. Having become interested in their conversations I turned to my brother Paul, who was more likely than any of the others to condescend to discuss these matters with me. He explained that Kerensky was a political opponent of my father and belonged to a diametrically opposed party. He went on to explain that Rasputin was considered a scoundrel who had slid into the confidence of the Empress Alexandra, because he, like nobody else, was able to heal the charming young heir, suffering from hemophilia. I was crushed by Paul's story since, like almost all Russian children, I adored the charming nine-year-old boy, whose portrait was hanging in my room. Something about his illness had come to me earlier, but for some reason it was surrounded with mystery and there was very little said about it.

At the beginning of 1914 we had a reception for members of the Duma, including Rodzyanko, the president of the Duma and Khvostov, a close friend of my father, who had been elected from the Nizhny-Novgorod province. There were many others whose names I did not know. From the conversation in my father's study, taking place over cocktails, I could hear that a great danger was threatening the country and that this danger for the most part was coming from a Siberain peasant—Rasputin—that very same man whom, exactly a year earlier, Rodzyanko had had thrown out of the Kazan Cathedral during the ceremonies celebrating the tricentennial of the Romanovs. Rasputin had been absent from St. Petersburg only a short while and was again playing a role at the court. Hating Rodzyanko, and not forgiving the insult, he apparently was taking his revenge now. For the first time that evening, there were conversations among the adults about the possibility of war. Having heard all this, I could not fall asleep for a long time—and when I did I had fearful nightmares depicting the little figure of the sick heir and above him the fearful, dark face of the bearded Rasputin.

## SUMMER 1914

Spring was wonderful that year, and as soon as school was out for the boys, we went to Obrochnoye. The last days in St. Petersburg were anxious. My parents were discussing the visit of Poincaré, happy over the alliance with France but fearing that this bore with it the possibility of war with Germany. They were speaking also about the frequent military parades taking place, for the most part, in Krasnoye Selo. The word "war" was heard more and more frequently. All of this made a vivid impression on my child's mind; I often would run to Paul, seeking answers for the questions troubling me. But he began to respond only with monosyllables and short answers. "If there will be a war, I will volunteer." And with that our conversations would end.

In Obrochnoye, when the relatives would gather and especially my two uncles Sergei and Nikolai, the shouting at Grandmother's house was incessant and could even be heard at our house. Father became exceptionally excited, not agreeing with his brothers' views. He was completely behind the reigning emperor, Nikolai II, while his brothers singled out the Tsaritsa Alexandra for attack and were irritated by the conduct of Rasputin.

Uncle Nikolai adored the Grand Prince Nikolai Nikolaevich and believed that he was the one who should be on the throne and not the weak-charactered Nikolai II, who was under the influence of his wife and Rasputin. Sergei was still more liberal and would shout about the necessity of a limitation on the power of the czar and the organization of a constituent assembly. My grandmother was horrified that everybody on the estate could hear these disputes between the brothers, and she implored them to quiet down. Quiet would reign for a short while, only to flare up again for some insignificant reason. I could not tolerate these meetings. They brought nothing but agitation and unpleasantness. When they occurred, I would take off to my dear horses and dogs and spend the rest of the day with them.

I remember as though it were today the bright, sunny day at the end of July when, having gathered all the girls, daughters of the workers and employees of the estate, I was putting on a play at the entryway. Soon we saw my brother Paul, galloping up the main road and turning toward the new house. He jumped from the saddle, and he seemed to be extremely upset about something. Tying up his horse, he went straight into the house. This was very unlike him. He would always stop in order to chat with my friends and me.

I sidled into the entryway and heard the conversation about the murder in Saraevo of Francis Ferdinand, [2] the nephew of the Austrian Emperor Franz Joseph. Paul was telling about an ultimatum sent by Austria to which Serbia was expected to reply in the course of forty-eight hours. "Now war is unavoidable," my father muttered. I jumped back to the porch in horror, stopped our play and sent the girls home.

Events began to unfold at an increased pace. In a few days Russia was already at war. Everywhere there was mobilization. In the nearest villages and in Obrochnoye there echoed the uninterrupted wailing of women and children who were seeing their husbands and fathers off to war.

At home the mood was tense. Paul, on the first day of the war, announced to my parents that he would quit the university and volunteer. Mother was in despair; having just recently lost her oldest son, she was afraid of being deprived of her second. My father was silent. Obviously there was a strong internal battle being waged; he could not but encourage the patriotic feelings of his son, but on the other hand he too was afraid of losing him. Paul had always been his favorite. The servants were also agitated. Almost every one of them had someone who had to go to fight. A general feeling of anxiety united them all; and a feeling of hatred flared up toward my governess, Ingeborg, who had returned to Obrochnoye with us that summer.

I remember one occurrence during this time of tension. At dinner when my family was present and Peter, the butler, was serving the food, I suddenly, and unexpectedly even for myself, turned to everybody and to nobody in particular with the question: "Is it true that our empress is a German?" As an answer to my question I was sent away not only from the table but also from the dining room by a deafening shout from my father. Covered with tears, I ran into my room and sobbed there for a long time, despite the attempts to console me by my mother and Ingeborg, who had come running to me. The unfairness of my father agitated me most of all.

"Indeed, everyone knows it," I kept repeating without pause, "everyone knows that the empress is a Darmstadt princess, and that means that she is a German." My father continued to rage for a long time in the dining room and we could hear my brothers trying to reassure him of something. Ingeborg, fearing that she would be suspected of holding such conversations with me, swore to Mother that she had nothing to do with it, that all the domestics beginning with Peter were speaking about it and that I heard such conversations everywhere. My mother, whose attitude was far less monarchist than my father's, did not attach any great significance to what had happened and only tried to convince me not to ask such questions in front of people and not to mix so much into affairs that did not concern me. With that the incident ended.

That fall our family went to St. Petersburg very early. Paul quit the university and entered the Nikolaevsky Cavalry Academy. Upon completion of his course work, he would go to war. He had already announced, under the obvious influence of Uncle Nikolai, that he would enter the Second Daghestan Cavalry Regiment. [3] Uncle Nikolai was also in that regiment and was great friends with Grand Prince Nikolai Nikolaevich. He knew the Grand Prince strongly favored the Daghestanys, so that it would be best if Paul would enter the Savage Regiment. Father was not satisfied with this, but Paul no longer wanted to think about anything else.

Every day everybody was following news from the front. Among our relatives and friends there were already sacrifices. The eldest son of Gershelman's aunt was killed. Vasya had lived with them until our move to St. Petersburg, and I too had stayed there for Easter when my parents had gone to Obrochnoye for the funeral. Gershelman had served in the Uhlan Regiment. From the first encounters with the enemy the regiment had suffered great losses. My cousin Sergei Davidov, who served in the Ismailovsky Regiment, had been wounded and was now in the hospital.

My parents let Ingeborg go. Since the beginning of the war her presence in our house had been unpleasant for everyone—and unpleasant for her too, I suspect. The adults often forgot about her and made various remarks which she involuntarily heard. The servants clearly were avoiding her. I emphatically anounced to Mother that I would not speak German on the streets. In recent days we had been walking in funeral silence, Ingeborg seething with irritation, but unable to do anything with me. Finally she herself could not put up with this situation any longer and asked my parents to release her. No one objected, and she left our home.

All of life in St. Petersburg had changed. Our happy dance classes had ceased; Colonel Gladky had left for war, and the parents of our classmates felt that now was not the time for dancing and for entertainment. I met my first love, Stepan, only rarely at the homes of mutual acquaintances. It seemed to me that he had completely changed. Last year I had been his main partner in dancing, and everyone had praised us. That had pleased him very much. Now, however, in these homes the girls were much older than I; they had common interests and secrets with Stepan, secrets that they tried very hard to conceal from me. I felt hurt and sad because of their scornful attitude toward me. One day I finally told my mother that I no longer wanted to go to those homes, since it was so boring. My first romance ended on that note.

Thirty-three years later, after the Second World War and while working as a secretary for the French in their Rhineland zone of occupation, I learned by chance that Stepan was living with his wife and child in Munich, in the American occupation zone. Since they knew neither English nor German, none of them could find employment. Through the director of the institution where I worked, I was able to get permission for them to come to the French zone. Since they all knew French very well, they had no trouble finding employment. During a conversation with me, Stepan had said that the winter of 1913–14, the dance classes at Gladky's, and his acquaintance with the little blue-eyed girl would always remain the bright spot of his life. (I was sorry I had not known that earlier.)

In the spring, my mother told me that we would not return to St. Petersburg the following winter but would spend it in Obrochnoye. That evening I was unable to fall asleep for a long time, trying to guess the reason for this decision. I kept wondering whether the Duma had been closed or whether my father was no longer in service. He was always in such an unpleasant mood, cursing Kerensky at every turn, and I surmised that Kerensky had most likely fired him.

Incidentally, my father always stated that Kerensky had a voice that squeaked when he would shout at meetings. Thirty-six years later, when I met this very same Kerensky in New York, I did not notice any squeaky voice. True, the circumstances had altered considerably. There was no one for him to shout at and no one with whom to quarrel. At this time he was assisting immigrants with obtaining loans from the bank with which he was associated. He also helped me. He seemed to be an extremely polite, elderly gentleman, gallantly holding my coat and opening the door. I was happy that it had not occurred to him to ask my maiden name, something that I am sure would have aroused in him the most unpleasant memories. Later, I again chanced to meet him on several occasions, even at a wedding of some mutual acquaintances; however, conversations about the past did not arise.

At home there were endless conversations about Rasputin, about the sick heir, and about the change of ministers. The conversations concerning the empress called forth great disagreement among the relatives. My father still tried to defend the czarist family; my mother, however, would maintain that Rasputin was a disgrace and that he would destroy the monarchy.

During this period in St. Petersburg, there was a great infatuation with spiritualism. My mother organized a circle of spiritualist devotees, who would often gather at our place. All the spirits summoned forth predicted the destruction of our state by Rasputin. I found these political séances extremely interesting, and I would try to enter the living room where they were taking place. But I would always be turned away.

The mood in Obrochnoye was so depressing that it seemed all joy had disappeared, never to return. [4] For whole days I ran around in the fields and forests or rode horseback. Austrian prisoners had been sent to work on the estate; and one of them, Wilhelm, worked as a stable-boy. He was given to me as a companion, since I was no longer satisfied with our hippodrome behind the estate but rode off into the neighboring villages and even into the huge pine forest about fifteen versts from our home. And only there, where I was able to gallop so that the wind whistled in my ear, was I able to forget everything that was happening around us all.

Summer came to a close and autumn arrived early. The question of my education arose; and my parents hired a young Russian teacher, Zinaida, from Murom. The young, modest, thin girl, about eighteen-years-old, soon appeared at our house. She had just finished the gymnasia and was highly recommended by our old family friend, a teacher in the Murom gymnasia. Everybody liked the girl, and we began our studies.

Late in the fall, in October, my parents decided to go to one of the Western provinces where the Daghestan Regiment had been sent for a rest. During their absence my old nana was called back from the country; they considered this young teacher too inexperienced and, moreover, a stranger in Obrochnoye. It was better to have one of our own Obrochnoye people at home. I was completely satisfied with this turn of affairs and had little regret over the departure of my parents.

In November my parents returned. The regiment's leave had ended. In the evenings my grandmother would come from the old house with her brother, and my parents would entertain everybody with stories about what had been taking place recently not far from the front. They had brought many photos with them and had made many new acquaintances. We began to look forward to Christmas and George's return.

Shortly before Christmas George and a *lycée* friend of his, Vorontsov-Dashkov, arrived. This Vorontsov was a handsome, red-cheeked boy of seventeen. He and George gave themselves over to all types of rural entertainment: skating down the hill, riding in the troika, skiing, etcetera. Their two-week stay in Obrochnoye meant nothing special to me personally; they considered me almost a child, treated me with disdain, and tried to avoid me at every turn. I of course was insulted and complained to Zinaida. She sympathized with me but could not help me.

In that year, 1915–16, my correspondence with a fourteen-year-old boy, the son of a friend of Mother's from Nizhny-Novgorod, served as my greatest entertainment. Every week, and especially on Tuesdays (apparently he wrote on Sundays), I would find that a small envelope with his letter was awaiting me at the post office. We exchanged news. He usually wrote about what was happening in the city, and I would describe our rural life.

In the spring of 1916, George transferred from the *lycée* to attend an accelerated curse in the Page Corps, in order to enter the artillery service. He intended to follow in the footsteps of Paul and go to war.

The summer of 1916 was not calm. The pleasant attitude of the local peasants changed, and various small disorders began to occur on the estate. Every Sunday boards from the fence separating the estate from the highway were broken. This highway led from Baev, the neighboring village, to the church in Obrochnoye. In the villages on the other side of the estate there was not one church for a distance of five versts; and, therefore, the peasants from these villages had to go past our estate. The summer was hot; the sun baked everything from early morning on. Of course it was more pleasant to walk along the dense birch path and not along the dusty road in the blazing sun. These trips through the park had formerly been forbidden by the manager, and no one had violated his edicts. Now, however, not only the youth but even older people took advantage of this break in the fence and went in whole crowds to the Obrochnoye church. No longer was anything effective. To my mother's great irritation, my father asked that we not interfere. He himself conversed with the elder of the church. For a time it appeared as though order had been reestablished—but not for long. Everything soon began again and with new force. The boards from the fence disappeared; the break kept growing larger, and the birch path was so trampled down that it looked as though a whole herd of cows had passed this way.

Sometimes strangers in civilian clothing would appear at the estate, and once they came and asked for Father. Father, as was his custom—he was always distinguished by his great hospitality—invited them to dinner. They were Mensheviks, who had often been in our area, and were interested in the mood of the peasants. At the table Father conversed with them quietly, which surprised me. But after their departure he was very upset and spoke for a long time with Mother, closing the doors of the living room. It was fortunate, at least, that there had been no scene in the presence of these strangers.

The longer this went on the more tense became the mood. Already there were suspicious persons in the country, making almost no attempt to hide and appearing at peasant gatherings. They would speak and arouse the peasants with their speeches. Sometimes they would fall into the hands of the police and were taken away, so it was said, to the Nizhny jail. For the most part, however, everything went smoothly for them; and they were left alone.

My friend from Nizhny wrote me that there too it was not calm. Rasputin was on everyone's lips. It was interesting that even my father had ceased to defend the tsarist family unconditionally, as he had formerly done. His hatred for Kerensky, however, did not abate; at every convenient opportunity he would again flare up and curse him up and down.

### CHRISTMAS 1916

The Christmas season came, and the huge Christmas tree was placed in the dining room. In Russia the first day is celebrated and not Christmas Eve. With my parents' permission, I had invited all the children not only of the local gentry but also our servants' children. The cook's daughter, my best friend, and I were preparing to entertain and treat them in every way possible. It was Christmas Eve. We were impatiently looking forward to the next day. Everybody gathered in the living room; my parents, Grandmother with her brother from the old house, my teacher Zinaida, and I were awaiting supper. According to the strict rules followed by Grandmother, eating was not permitted until the first star of Christmas Eve appeared.

It was then that a noise was heard in the antechamber; the outside door opened, someone entered, and voices rose in the hall. I was the first to break away and rushed to meet the unexpected guests. In the doorway leading to the dining room, I froze with surprise and joy.

In the hall, wearing a fur jacket, a Caucasian fur cap, and covered by a scarlet cape, stood my brother Paul. In a second I was embracing him, and right behind me all the others came rushing. During the kissing and the questioning no one noticed that in the corner there was a small figure patiently waiting. Paul, breaking away from the embraces of the family, introduced his friend Victor Stein. He had already written to us about him, and now he had brought him home for his leave.

From that day on entertainment alternated between our house and those of our neighbors, where there would be a large gathering of guests. In the daytime we would ride on horses in the surrounding areas or go sleighriding on the icy slopes on the estate itself. Victor turned out to be a cheerful, witty fellow. Every day he would think up something new. He amused himself like a child; and, indeed, he was all of nineteen years old.

We welcomed in the New Year at our neighbors', the Priklonskys. Their village, Ulyanovka, was only three versts from Obrochnoye. For Paul's and Victor's entertainment the young teachers, the Chizhovys, had been invited. There were seven of those girls, between the ages of eighteen and twenty-seven. My favorite was the twenty-year-old Shurochka, who was in love with my brother Paul. That evening everybody forgot about the war, and about the fact that soon Paul and Victor would have to return to the front. We were merry as never before. It seems to me now that that was the last such carefree, tempestuous party.

A few days later news of the murder of Rasputin reached us. In our house there was general happiness and the hope that now everything should change for the better. But our hopes for favorable changes were not realized. The agitation did not subside. Events began to unfold with unbelievable speed, and for us there was already nothing pleasant and happy at the beginning of 1917.

Early one morning in the beginning of February, Zinaida came into my room, pale and looking frightened. I was not sleeping, but I was still lying in my bed. I looked up at her in amazement; but before I could utter a word I heard the frightful words, "Get up quickly, your grandmother has been burned! Your parents spent the night in the old house." She told me how it had happened. Grandmother had gone to the bathroom that night with a candle, there being no electricity in the old house. She had put the candle on the floor and apparently had dozed off. She came to with her long woolen robe in flames. Anushka, the maid who was sleeping next door, came running at her scream; and with her sister's help—Grandmother was raising two orphan sisters—tore off the robe and wrapped Grandmother in wet linen. At the same time the girls were successful in putting out the fire in the robe and several other things also reached by the flames; and they then sent for my parents. A doctor was called immediately from the village of Kemlya, about five versts from Obrochnoye. Another doctor, for whom horses had been sent to the county seat, arrived early in the morning. After examining Grandmother he announced that the burns were third-degree and there was almost no hope for her recovery.

From that day until the 27th of February, the day of Grandmother's death, there was not a minute of peace for my parents, for the relatives who had gathered, or for the servants. But the most painful suffering fell, of course, to Grandmother. I can remember that no matter where I went the pitiful, even whining, voice of my unfortunate grandmother would follow me. Only in the evening, after a tormenting bandaging, would they give her sedatives; and for a little while she would fall into not quite a sleep but a semiconscious condition.

My mother and aunt, my father's sister who had just arrived from Simbirsk, took turns caring for Grandmother. To Grandmother it seemed that Mother gave the best care, and she asked for her to stay there all the time. After a few days it was difficult to recognize Mother; she had grown pale and so thin that it had painfully pinched her pretty features.

Grandmother's face did not suffer at all. When she was laid to rest on the 27th of February, everyone was amazed by how young, peaceful, and pretty she looked. Before the funeral the nuns from the neighboring convent arrived. It had been Grandmother's desire that a choir of nuns would sing her funeral litany. Formerly she had visited this convent often, and she liked the nuns' singing very much.

The entire old house was filled with black figures gliding silently over the parquet floor. The abbess herself, a fat, tall, handsome woman, conducted everything. And indeed they sang wonderfully; the beautiful voices filled the entire house. "It's as though angels are carrying away your grandmother's soul," said Nana.

The many funeral services, the nuns' singing, the smell of incense, and the innumerable burning candles had such an effect on me that on the second day I fainted during the service, frightening Mother, who could hardly stand on her feet herself. I was sent to the new house and forbidden to come any more. Futhermore, despite my entreaties and tears, I was not taken to the burial. And thus our energetic, happy grandmother, a pillar of the old regime, departed.

At this time in distant St. Petersburg events were unfolding, [5] events that would reflect not only on our future but also on the future of the entire nation. We had already heard about the czar's abdication; but, suffering the horror of Grandmother's illness, even Father had reacted with indifference. Now, however, revolution was stirring throughout the land.

Grandmother was buried on the 1st of March. A multitude of relatives and friends arrived, and the procession stretched from the estate to the church. Grandmother's favorite nephew, Uhlan Denis Davidov, came from the front. Later on I was told that he had requested that he be photographed at the doors to the crypt into which the coffin was lowered. I saw this photograph; he was standing with bowed head, in deep sorrow. In a month he himself was killed at the front.

The evening after the burial Father said, as if to himself, not turning to anyone in particular, "With Mama they have buried the old world. This world has gone forever. What does the future have in store for us?"

Not even two weeks had passed since the day of the funeral when a whole crowd of Obrochnoye and Baev peasants, headed by representatives of the local authority, came looking for my uncle Sergei, who was supposedly in hiding. He had been the leader of the Penza gentry; and the peasants disliked him very much, even though he was a liberal. Strangely enough, my father, a fervent monarchist, was greatly respected and liked by the peasants.

Then the crowd began to go through our house, looking in all corners, even under the beds. The women, taking advantage of the occasion to roam through the "lord's chambers," were in ecstasy over the mirrored dressers that reflected in natural size; they tried to strum on the piano and were especially impressed by the marble bath in my mother's bedroom. They did not take anything, despite the fact that much of it must have been attractive to them. I mixed in with the crowd, which was full of my childhood acquaintances. Nobody drove me out; but, on the contrary, they asked me about various objects they were seeing for the first time. Most of all I was amused by two countrywomen when they dragged out a chamber pot, wondering whether it was a pot for making soup. The search ended without any results. Of course they were unable to find Sergei; he had not been at our place since the funeral. The peasant elders excused themselves for the inconvenience they had caused and shook Father's hand. There was no hostility shown toward him even from the younger ones.

Soon we learned that Uncle had been found and put into prison. Auntie was busy trying to obtain his release; and their daughter Natasha, about ten years old, had been sent to us and put into my room. Father was in a depressed state all this time. He could not reconcile himself to the fact that besides Prince Lvov, his most inveterate foe, Kerensky, was also in the Provisional government.

The amusing thing was that every single one of the women teachers whom we kept meeting was in love with Kerensky. My Zinaida was no exception. But knowing my father's attitude, she avoided conversations on this subject. I discovered by chance a photograph of Kerensky in her most cherished redoubt, a small suitcase that she opened at times in order to go through her treasures. Catching sight of me, she quickly tried to hide it; but I had already seen everything and for a long time after that I teased her. She begged me not to tell my parents.

I continued my correspondence with my Nizhny friend, Aleksei, sharing our impressions of what was occurring, each one of us solemnly announcing to the other that "I, of course, am on the side of the insurgents." Aleksei, moreover, announced that he was going around with a red band and advised me to do the same. Nonetheless, I refused, fearing my father's reaction.

In May of that year my mother and I were supposed to go to Nizhny, where I had to take the exams for the gymnasium instead of the institute, as we had earlier intended. I was enjoying the anticipation of this trip, but we were first awaiting the arrival of George and two of his friends for the Easter holidays. On Monday of Holy Week the young men arrived late in the evening, when Natasha and I were already asleep. In the morning Zinaida, happy and excited, burst into my room announcing the arrival of the young men and began to chatter of the impressions the young fellows had made on her. It seems that she had fallen in love immediately with all three.

From that day, my father did everything possible to entertain our guests. Horseback riding was followed by hunting and then by fishing. At the same time, church services, so important during Holy Week, were not omitted. There was time for everything, and the young ones suffered from only one thing—the Lenten food, with its absence of meat. This, of course, had been our custom since time immemorial.

On the other hand, what a celebration it was when, after the midnight service (because of George and his friends Father broke the long-standing rule of standing throughout the entire service until almost four o'clock in the morning) everyone arrived home and was struck by the sight of the table already prepared. It was sagging under a huge quantity of dishes. Everything was there—a whole pig, a whole ham, veal, all types of hors d'oeuvres, paskhi, kulichi, decorated eggs, and, most important of all, a whole series of drinks of our own brew.

The young men remained two weeks at our house; and during that time they won quite a few hearts among the local young ladies and the young servants. Not to mention my modest Zinaida, and me. For a long time the image of the attractive nineteen-year-old Cadet Nikita Zubov remained in my imagination, entirely crowding out memories of my first love, my blue-eyed Stepan.

Since I was sometimes allowed to ride horseback with them, Nikita, noticing my silent adoration, gave me a riding stick with a silver knob engraved with my initials. I carefully preserved this gift and took it everywhere with me until 1942—until that day when we left our cold, starving, besieged Leningrad. That was the first time that I neglected even to think about taking this precious thing with me.

After the departure of the young men, my mother and I spent two weeks in Nizhny. I successfully passed the exams and, while there, underwent minor foot surgery as well. June, July, and August slipped past comparatively quietly. We had few quests; Grandmother's death and Uncle Sergei's arrest gave little reason for merriment.

Toward the end of August, Mama received a telegram from her sister, Aunt Liza, asking permission to come to Obrochnoye with her husband and daughter and remain with us for the winter. They were living in Chausyi, in the Mogilev province. There had been constant unrest there, and they preferred to go deeper into the country where it seemed safer to them.

The first of September our family grew with the arrival of my aunt, uncle, and cousin Marina. I was overjoyed by their arrival. It seemed to me the tense atmosphere that had not left our house would now be dispersed. I was mistaken in this. Aunt and Uncle, frightened by the revolution, spoke of nothing else and dragged Mama into their political concerns. Under their influence, she began to look at many things with completely different eyes.

My cousin and I spent all our time outside the house. I tried to entice her to go horseback riding but, unfortunately, without success. Having lived her whole life in the city, she had had little contact with the animal world and neither my favorite dogs nor horses could attract her in any way. She agreed only to ride the troikas. Thus, our favorite entertainments were trips to the distant forest for the mushrooms that were especially abundant this year.

September and a large part of October went by uneventfully. But the Bolshevik Revolution of October 25, 1917 made itself felt on all of us. The smashing and looting of estates began, accompanied by fires; and one of the first estates attacked was that of our neighbor, Priklonsky. They were looking for him and apparently wanted to kill him. However, he and his family had long since left the area. Only ashes were left of his house. The estate of the Filosophous, about five versts from us, was also burned.

The most alarming rumors were coming from everywhere. My teacher Zinaida, frightened to death, requested that we let her go; and at the first opportunity she went home to Murom. My father refused to move anywhere, convinced that no one would touch him. In this conviction he was supported by the Obrochnoye peasantry and especially by the older ones. Their relationship with Father was unusually good. So many times the manager, and even Mother, had reproached Father for his kindness and wastefulness. My father would always joke and say that he had enough for his lifetime and that of his sons, and that he would give his daughter in marriage to a rich man so that she would need no dowry. Joking or not, it seemed that this was true and that no danger threatened. But now, toward evening, a few carts appeared on the big road dividing the estate, going in the direction of the old house. Nobody was living in the old house except the two sisters, watching the remains of Grandmother's property. The frightened girls ran to us, telling us how the crowd had smashed in the doors and shutters. A complete pillaging of the house was taking place. Indeed, soon the shouts and sounds of smashing glass were carried to our house. A delegation of peasants, headed by the village elders, called for my father. They advised us all to leave our house, promising to guard it and the estate from further destruction. They said that the pillaging of the old house had been done not by our Obrochnoye peasants but by peasants from other villages, and they could not, of course, guarantee anything in that regard. My father would under no circumstances agree to leave our estate, but he did decide to send the women and us girls away. A huge, robust fellow, one of our Obrochnoye peasants, was sent to accompany us. He gathered up our huge suitcases where the most essential things had hastily been packed, as though they were feathers. We headed in the direction of the station where we were supposed to move in with the stationmaster, an old friend of my father's. While we were leaving, almost without interruption, the roar of voices and the noise and crashing from the direction of the old house could be heard.

It was fearful to think what would happen if that band would abandon its pillaging and come after us. This fear was ungrounded. No one was interested in us; obviously they were too much attracted by the booty from our old house, with its furniture, porcelain, clothes, and the other things accumulated over centuries. The stationmaster took us in; and it was from that day, the 27th of October 1917, that our nomadic life began.

My father remained a few more days on the estate, surrounded day and night by peasants faithful to him. My uncle, who had arrived from Chausyi, and my grandmother's brother remained with him. Both of them were uneasy and strongly tried to persuade my father to leave. He continued his stubborn refusal, and Mother announced that she would not leave without him.

We were supposed to head for Lukoyanov. Almost all the regional gentry had already arrived there. Every day we heard rumors about new pogroms, fires, and even murders. I wanted to leave Obrochnoye as quickly as possible and tried, as hard as I could, to persuade Father when he would come to visit us on his one remaining horse. All of our horses and cattle had been carried off the first night after the pillaging of the old house. Only after ten days did Father agree to leave. Our benefactors brought us a few extra things from the house, and on the 12th of November 1917 we left Obrochnoye forever.

*EDITOR'S NOTES*

1. Rasputin, a virtually illiterate peasant from a Siberian village and an adherent of an outlawed religion, had come to the capital in 1905. Although he wore the robes of a Russian holy man, causing many outsiders to think he was a monk, he had never been ordained. In the early years of the century, spiritualism and other types of supernatural fads were in vogue in certain social circles in St. Petersburg and other world centers such as London. In the capital Rasputin gained some renown as a holy man who worked miracles. At this time the Empress had one son. The heir to the Russian throne suffered from hemophilia, a condition against which the best doctors available could do nothing. Rasputin was presented to the Empress by several socialite duchesses, and he made a very favorable impression. Through reasons never clearly understood, although hypnotism is strongly indicated, Rasputin was able to alleviate the Tsarevich's condition, something the doctors could not do. Unflattering reports about Rasputin and his personal conduct were not believed by the Empress who was used to false, unsavory, and malicious reports concerning persons around the throne. Thus, even true accounts about scandals involving Rasputin were not believed by the Empress who attributed them to slander for personal reasons. Rasputin's presence around the throne became something of a scandal. The czar, pressured by his ministers, ordered Rasputin to leave the capital. However, scarcely had Rasputin departed when the Tsarevich had another serious attack of hemophilia, and again the palace doctors proved ineffectual. A hurried call brought Rasputin to the phone, and he was able to improve the boy's condition by talking with him. Rasputin returned to the palace; henceforth, the Empress would not hear of his being ordered away. During the war, when the czar had left for headquarters, Rasputin was able to exert an enormous influence on all types of governmental appointments, a situation that did much to erode respect for the royal family. The honest and capable ministers of the government detested him as did Rodzyanko, the president of the Duma. Here in her accounts, Elena recalls an incident one year before the war when Rodzyanko was able to order Rasputin's removal from the cathedral.
2. The murder in June 1941 of Austrian Archduke Francis Ferdinand, the heir to the Austrian throne, was the catalyst which began World War I. The outraged Austrians, blaming Serbia for having permitted and encouraged the terrorist-nationalist organizations from whose ranks the assassins

had come, presented the Serbians an ultimatum and a number of demands. On July 28, 1914 Austria declared war on Serbia, hoping that the pledge of German support would keep Russia out of the war and that Austria would have a free hand with Serbia. On July 29, Russia ordered general mobilization. In 1914 mobilization by a great power was considered virtually the same as a declaration of war. The Germans felt that if Russia were to be allowed all the time needed to mobilize armies and bring men up to the frontier, Russia's enormous superiority in manpower, especially when supported by the French with whom the Russians had an alliance, would make a German defeat inevitable. Once Russia ordered mobilization, the war could not be stopped. Actually, the seeds for this war had been sown in 1871. For in 1871, Prussia, victorious in the war with France, had taken the two frontier provinces of Alsace and Lorraine and annexed them to the newly proclaimed German Empire. French resentment at the loss of these provinces poisoned German-French relations during the next forty years. It was to keep France from finding allies that German Chancellor Bismarck concluded alliances with other European states, particularly Austria and Russia, in the 1870s and 1880s. Young Kaiser Wilhelm, however, allowed the treaty with Russia to lapse in 1890; and within four years France had succeeded in concluding an alliance with Russia. Continental Europe was thus divided into the two military alliances that led to the World War of 1914. The visits to Russia of French Premier Poincaré in August of 1912 and July of 1914, mentioned by Elena, were goodwill missions intended to reinforce the Franco-Russian alliance.

3.   The Daghestan Cavalry Regiment, sometimes referred to as the Savage Regiment, was an elite outfit and remained loyal to the government long after others had dissolved.

4.   World War I opened very badly for Russia. The Russians, anxious to divert the Germans from their swift advance toward Paris, ignored their long-prepared war plans that called for an orderly mobilization and build-up on the front and prematurely launched a great push into Germany's eastern province of East Prussia. There at Tannenberg they sufferd one of the worst military defeats in history. Russian losses in this one battle were over a quarter of a million men and a good part of the heavy artillery. After Tannenberg every battery in the Russian army was reduced from six to four guns. War was thus brought home to Russia and to hundreds of thousands of Rusian families at virtually the very outset.

5.   In the winter of 1916-17 the war situation had worsened for the Russians. The rumors about Rasputin's scandalous conduct had hurt the prestige of the royal family. All types of corruption had been uncovered in government. Wages were not keeping pace with inflation. Russia, which had mobilized the largest army in world history, had suffered the greatest military casualties in world history. The Russian rail system, unable to keep up with the added burdens of war, was increasingly breaking down. By March 1917 supply problems had caused food shortages in the capital. Bread lines were forming before the bakeries. Demonstrations against the czar's government began to occur. After several days of demonstrations the troops in the capital no longer attempted to disperse the mobs; some even went over to the demonstrators. The czar abdicated, and more than a

thousand years of monarchy in Russia came to an end. A provisional government became nominally the executive authority in Russia. This provisional government held power, however, only with the approval of the Soviets (Councils) of Workers and Soldiers Deputies which had been established in the capital and were rapidly being set up in all major Russian cities. It was at this juncture in history that the fire occurred in Elena's grandmother's house.

# 2

# ADOLESCENT YEARS

## *LUKOYANOV*

On a gloomy November day, we Obrochnoye exiles arrived in the small provincial town of Lukoyanov. I had never been there before, and it made a most unpleasant impression on me. From the station there extended a very long muddy road with little wooden huts along both sides. It went to the so-called center, consisting of a square with a cathedral surrounded on all four sides by various buildings occupied by city administrative workers and two or three stores with the most pitiful show windows. Father, who had often visited Lukoyanov in the past, told us about the city's history and the changes that had taken place there.

We went to Father's former secretary, who had been able to adapt to the new order and yet preserve good relations with the "former people," such as my father. He offered us two rooms in his rather spacious apartment. However, despite the best of intentions, it was rather difficult to make room for our entire family. With the two servants, we numbered nine persons. Fortunately, Ephimov had thought about this and arranged with the priest in the neighboring street to give us three rooms and the summer (outdoor) kitchen of his own house. The women, my mother, aunt, Cousin Marina, and the two servants, moved in at Father Basil's, where we were warmly welcomed by him and his wife. To some degree this made it easier for us to adapt to the somber November weather and the unfamiliar, forbidding city in which we now had to live.

Days passed—days not at all like those in Obrochnoye. Most of all I missed my beloved horseback riding through the fields and meadows surrounding the estate. Instead of our large manorial home, we now lived in a small apartment. Instead of a huge park, there was a small garden twenty paces in length through which, nevertheless, Marina and I would walk twenty or thirty minutes for the sake of exercise, sharing our impression that this reminded us of a prison courtyard where the prisoners are exercised. To roam around town was no great pleasure.

The residents mostly stayed at home—these were uneasy times, and every day there were new measures of oppression from the Soviet government. The weather also was not good; it was a cold, damp November with strong winds and frequent rains. The food situation was poor. The local inhabitants were still living off old supplies and the produce from their gardens and orchards. But it was extremely difficult for all the newcomers, and there were many of them in Lukoyanov. All the landowners, not only of Lukoyanov but also of the surrounding districts, for some reason chose to gather in this town. Every day we found out that others had arrived, and the population continued to grow. Marina and I liked this, because it was interesting to make new acquaintances. Many had children of our age with whom we quickly became friends. We began to put on children's shows; we even organized dance lessons. Classes were begun on various subjects: mathematics, geography, history, botany, and foreign languages. Uncle taught the more serious subjects, and Mother began to give us French and Russian language lessons. She especially tormented us with grammar, toward which neither of us felt any attraction. Thus, all of November and half of December passed without incident.

One evening in the latter part of December, when Marina and I were carefully preparing our lessons for the next day, there was a thundering knock at the front door. We both jumped up, and in a second I was hanging around the neck of my brother Paul.

It seems that Paul, having been released from military service, had gone home to Obrochnoye. When the train approached the station, he overheard a conversation between two men in the corridor. One of them, pointing to Father's estate as the train was passing, said to the other, "And there is the former estate of Gorstkin." Paul overheard these remarks and was struck by the word "former." He began to converse with the stranger and learned that about two months previously the estate had been seized by the peasants; the old house was burned and the landowners had gone to Lukoyanov. Not getting off at the stop, Paul rode on further and easily found us in Lukoyanov.

Everyone crowded around him, asking about the situation at the front, about his personal affairs, and telling him about the events we had all endured. The joy of the meeting was darkened by these events and by our wretched circumstances. How different this all was from his arrival in Obrochnoye at Christmas only one year earlier.

A few days later George arrived. Since he had been in Petrograd, my parents were able to inform him of our new location and he came directly to us.

Now the question of looking for another apartment became more acute. Thanks to the energetic efforts of my brothers, by the first of January we had moved to Pokrovsky Street. Marina and I called this street the Nevsky Prospekt, for it was the widest and best in town; moreover, in the evening much of the younger population would stroll here, get acquainted, and set dates for future meetings. In spite of our extreme youth, we would also walk there every evening—to the great displeasure of both my mother and my strict aunt. Nonetheless, under various pretenses we would manage to sneak out after supper and stroll for at least an hour.

Right after vacation Marina and I were accepted by a school located in the large red building on the main square, opposite the cathedral. But Marina's extremely reactionary parents took her out of school almost immediately. They found that the instruction was not being conducted in the same manner to which they had become accustomed in pre-revolutionary Russia; however, what irritated them most was that the children had to do the janitorial work. Every Saturday we either loaded wood (essential not only for our school but for all municipal organizations) or, if we remained in town, washed all the huge windows and scrubbed the floors of the classrooms and the corridors. The children, not all accustomed to such work, got very tired and often, the next day if the work had been on Sunday, were unable to attend the lessons at school. Of course these girls were subjected to all types of ridicule, not only from their fellow students but also from some of the teachers who were trying to adapt to the new regime.

Despite the fact that I had engaged in a lot of sports, loved to work in the orchard and garden, and rode horseback, the carrying of the very heavy wood and scrubbing the concrete floors often was too much for me. In my class there was a strong, healthy girl Marfushka, from one of the neighboring villages, who was acustomed to all types of household work. Marfushka felt a great sympathy for me and offered the following exchange: she would wash the windows and floors and I would help her with the French that gave her trouble no matter how hard she tried. My salvation was found. Soon Marfushka began to receive good marks instead of her usual D's; I, however, would write various exercises and short compositions on Saturdays that she would pick up the same day, rewrite, and give to our teacher. The teacher, Maria Ivanovna, also from the gentry newcomers to Lukoyanov, was happy to grab the first position available; and she was not especially interested in details of how Marfushka had developed such a talent for foreign languages. Obviously she attributed this all to her own instruction and praised Marfushka at teachers' meetings. My absence from the "Saturdays" went unnoticed for a rather amusing reason. At that time my brother had also taken a position as teacher of Latin at our school. George was exceptionally handsome, tall, and well-built. All the young teachers fell in love with him. He in turn was nice to all and showed no preference. This was my salvation. Obviously, each one of these girls was hoping to win his heart and would avoid making any trouble for a younger sister who had broken school regulations. In addition, it might also be noted that at that time there was no real order and control in the schools.

Toward spring the preparation of wood and the scrubbing of floors ceased. It was no longer necessary to heat the quarters, and the pupils had done such a poor job of scrubbing and cleaning that the administration decided to hire two healthy scrubwomen entrusted with keeping order in the school building.

All this was my good fortune; otherwise, they would not have accepted my absences and the substitutions. Actually, my French teacher, Maria Ivanovna, was head over heels in love with my handsome brother and being extremely energetic and having had a great deal of experience in matters of love—she had already been married and divorced—had dispersed all of his modest and timid worshippers by declaring her indisputable claims to him. Of course this created some irritation and discussion among our teachers, and my situation was extremely shaky. There could no longer be any hope of their being indulgent to me. But now, thanks to the new directives of the administration, I no longer needed their laxness. Insofar as classes were concerned, I studied well; and there was no need for anyone to find fault with me. However, for old times sake I continued to help Marfushka with her difficult French so she too did not suffer from the changes that occurred. I had entered into my new role of teacher and would not have wished to turn her down, which later apparently influenced the career I chose.

Summer returned and again brought various changes into our lives. I frequently heard Father converse with my brothers about their leaving Lukoyanov. For the time being this was limited only to talk; but in the middle of June, noting the concerned look on my mother's face, I asked her what was happening. She replied that Father and Paul were leaving and that George would remain with us for now.

### GEORGE'S ARREST AND AN OUTBREAK OF TYPHUS

After the departure of Father and Paul, Mother again began to look for an apartment, this time for a smaller one; for both Uncle and Auntie, along with Marina, had moved to the country with one of Uncle's pupils. Uncle was seriously engaged in teaching that brought him, in addition to the money that was losing all its value, food in exchange for lessons.

Soon Mother found a two-room apartment on the same street where we had lived earlier, and toward the beginning of the school year we moved there. George continued to teach Latin in our school and that year I was his student. I gained nothing at all from the fact that the teacher was my brother; on the contrary, I lost. At first I thought that the study of Latin was not worthwhile and that it would be better to study the other subjects. But, having received a "D" on my first work, I understood that I could no longer fool around with my brother. I had to make up what I had missed posthaste, and, as a result, this miserable Latin was taking up all my time.

Fall arrived, and it became cold as the days grew shorter. Life again took on a regular routine. For me the days were flying past imperceptibly and even happily. The school, the music lessons given me by one of my friends, the evening get-togethers where we put on plays and other programs (after which we danced in the large room of the old school building), all made life interesting.

But toward the end of October a wave of arrests began. The first to be taken was an elderly magnate from the neighboring district who had settled here with his family a year ago. In the morning, before my departure for school, his wife ran to our place. Very much upset and in tears, she told us the bad news and asked for advice as to what to do in those circumstances.

Two days scarcely passed before both Messing brothers were arrested. A panic began in town. There were twelve families of former landowners in Lukoyanov at that time; and every day, first one, then another was arrested. Terrified, we awaited our turn.

In the beginning of November one midnight when we had already been sleeping a long time, a deafening knock sounded on the door. George went out to open it. At least ten armed men burst into the room. Not presenting any documents and threatening him with their revolvers, although George did not offer any resistance whatsoever, they announced that George was under arrest. They yelled at Mother, who, greatly agitated, demanded from them a warrant for the arrest or at least an explanation. I was standing in the corner, trembling from fear and looking with horror at this band of coarse, dirty people in ragged caps and tattered overcoats, people who were unceremoniously going through our apartment, taking with them everything they could lay their hands on. They even took away my first earnings: a little ring set with a turquoise that I had received as pay for lessons I had given to a girl.

They took George away. My mother and I remained alone. I was shaking and sobbing, overwhelmed with fear for my brother and anxious about all of us. This was the first direct collision with the new regime. What could we expect from them? Indeed, this was a crowd of real bandits.

In half an hour our neighbor, having heard everything but fearing to show any sign of life, rushed into our apartment. Her father had formerly served in the police, and although he had had a very minor post, he was nonetheless expecting that any day now they would seize him and throw him into jail.

My mother, a woman of strong character, energetic, and intelligent, did not know how to cry. She bore quietly all the trials fate had sent her, and many thought she was a heartless and cold person, however, I knew that this was not so. That night, having poured me an extra large portion of "Valerinki" and put me to bed, she did not lie down but went through everything the bandits left: letters, papers, and my diaries.

When I woke up in the morning, the only thing she said to me was, "How fortunate that they didn't take your diaries." Being a modest and reserved person, she had never read either my letters or my notes. I could understand the horror she must have experienced that night when she read my observations about the undesirability, and the danger, of the counterrevolutionary activity of my father, who was dreaming of rescuing the czar and the royal family by taking them out of Siberia. Having accidentally heard my parents' conversation on that theme, and knowing my mother's relationship to her favorite son whom she so feared losing, I had not hesitated entering my impressions in my diary. And soon, since nothing had come of my father's plans, I had even forgotten that I had written about it. Now I understood perfectly that had my diaries fallen into the hands of the Chekists, George would have been shot without hesitation. Two thick notebooks with my writings were burned that night.

In the afternoon my cousin came running and informed us that that very night her husband and two of her brothers had been arrested. She was expecting her first child. She had become so distraught from the arrest of those dear to her, and from the search that had lasted several hours, that a doctor had to be called. Only now that she had recovered a bit did she come to tell us her sad news. Poor Mother! On top of everything else, she now had to calm this young woman, promising to help her and to take on the care of two children, her nephews, who were now without supervision.

The arrests continued, and during the next few days almost all the men who belonged to our circle of friends were taken. All the "suspicious" inhabitants of the city were placed in the jammed city jail, along with them.

Mother obtained a pass to see George and, having yielded to my persistent entreaties, took me with her. It was early in the morning on a sunny and cold November day that my mother, my cousin Xenia, and I traveled out of town to the prison. When we arrived, women were already standing in a long line, awaiting their meetings. Among them were many of our acquaintances. We were taken to a narrow rectangular room, and they began to call out the prisoners.

Such a murmur arose in response to the disorder and shouting of the jailors, that it was almost impossible to make anything out! Finally they brought in our George. Upon seeing him, pale, thin, and unshaven, I seized my mother's arm in horror and could not say even one word. She, however, did not succumb to the impression that my brother had undoubtedly made on her and greeted him animatedly, even cheerfully. I could only be astounded at her willpower and amazing character. All around us there were agitated voices and the sound of sobbing, interrupted by the shouts of the guards. Mother exchanged several words with George, trying to encourage him and give him hope of a quick release. I was certain that her firm and cheerful appearance raised his spirits. But we left supporting Xenia under both arms. She was sobbing harshly. The sight of her husband, agitated and pitiful, had a devastating effect on her; and, instead of cheering him up as my mother had done with George, she had burst out crying.

We were later joined by other friends who shared with us their hopes and plans for the release of their dear ones. However, a completely unexpected event did more to help than all our efforts and attempts to obtain a fair judgment in the upper echelons of the new government. In the jail an outbreak of typhus flared up. The filth, the overcrowding, the insects—all had helped spread the disease. The hospital was filled to overflowing. Violent criminals were transferred to the old half-ruined building near the station. Our people, however, whose crime consisted for the most part only in that they belonged to the bourgyie (bourgeois) class, as they were then called, were released.

The city rejoiced, forgetting the reason for the release of the prisoners, a reason which did not presage anything good. And, indeed, in a very short time typhus began to appear among those released. The first victim was the elderly Mr. Zyikov, the husband of my mother's friend. Since there was no room in the hospital, he lay at home; and in spite of the care of his wife and sister-in-law, he died after a few days. The elder brother of Xenia's husband also became ill, and he also had to be taken to the cemetery. Others, the younger ones, fought the disease that was now taking on the character of an epidemic.

Twelve days after his release from prison, our George also came down with typhus. Even Mother, in spite of amazing strength, began to look desperate. The doctor, our old acquaintance, was visiting regularly, prescribing necessary medicines that, as a rule, were not to be had in the pharmacy. The main misfortune, however, was the total absence of all essential foods that could reinforce my brother's constitution, weakened by his stay in prison.

Mother watched over him day and night, not allowing me near. When he would fall asleep, she would run to the neighbors, imploring them to obtain food products in exchange for the valuables she had managed to preserve and that she now gave eagerly for the necessary butter, eggs, and milk. The old doctor presented her with two bottles of cognac. It was then that I saw tears in her eyes.

Now each day I was delegated to beat the egg yolks and mix them with cognac. George took this drink several times a day. In a month Mother had cured him completely, and neither she nor I got infected. But George did not return to our school; he was inducted into the Red Army, and he left Lukoyanov.

A change was also awaiting me. Because of the absence of fuel, all the lower classes up to the fifth, were closed. The girls' school and the boys' high school were joined. I was in the fourth class, so for me there arose the important question of how I would continue my education. Having discussed this with Mother, I said that during the vacation—from the 1st to the 15th of January—I would try to cover the entire year's program and enter into the fifth class.

A remarkable bracelet of turquoise surrounded by diamonds that I had always admired in childhood, and that had been promised to me when I would marry, was sacrificed for this. Since it was still long before this event, the bracelet was used for a more real and essential purpose. Mother went to the country, where her sister lived, and there she successfully exchanged the bracelet for such a quantity of food that it saved us from the approaching famine and made it possible for us to pay for three teachers, with whom I immediately began to study diligently.

I shall probably never forget those lessons. There was no kerosene and all the lamps were out of service; the only thing that served for illumination was little "koptilka," as they were called. They were made by pouring kerosene into a saucer and inserting a wick. This apparatus would be placed right under the nose, and then one could read only with difficulty. January is a dark month, and it was necessary to study from morning until late at night. Nonetheless, we succeeded in overcoming all difficulties; and in the middle of January, to my unbelievable joy, I was accepted into the fifth class. Among the students of the fifth class were many former friends and acquaintances. But mainly I was proud that I had overcome a difficult obstacle and had become one year older.

Spring arrived. This is a wonderful time in central Russia. The snow melted, noisy rivulets ran, the innumerable gardens and orchards turned green and simply seemed to drown the city in their verdure. Soon the city park and summer theater, closed for the winter, opened. The main thing, which is the unbelievable charm of Russia, the country and the provinces—the nightingales sang. Nightingales were everywhere—in the smallest gardens, in the city park, and in the grove adjacent to the city. Their singing cannot be compared to anything. It reminded me ever so strongly of Obrochnoye, where each spring, as soon as it would get dark, the trilling of the nightingales would start in our park. In spite of the fact that we did not know anything at all about the fate of Papa and Paul, and in spite of the constantly growing famine and disorder in a country being torn apart by civil war and terror of the government, often everything was forgotten; and we, especially the young ones, would enjoy the awakening of nature, the singing of the birds, the green of the grass and the flowers, and—we began to hope for something better in our lives.

In the spring our George came home for a few days. He had been appointed to a purchasing commission, acquiring horses for the Red Army. This time he had been assigned to our region, and he could spend some time with us. His service friend, Sergei Skrjabin, came with him. This young soldier made no impression on me, and apparently this feeling was mutual. I was so much younger than the Lukoyanov ladies whom the young men were courting that it was impossible for me to compete with them. At that time no one could have foreseen that five years later I would become the wife of this soldier who was ignoring me then because of my age.

During these days of George's stay with us, Mother was completely transformed. Her favorite had come home healthy, cheerful, happy, and having become a really handsome fellow.

In addition, George told us that he soon would be transferred to Simbirsk and that he wanted to take us with him. This prospect cheered up Mother even more, but it saddened me. I had already become accustomed to Lukoyanov and had many friends there. I loved my school. The prospect of giving all this up did not appeal to me at all. In two weeks our studies would end; and the advanced classes, to which I now belonged, would go to Nizhny-Novgorod to see the city, visit the theaters, and other attractions. If we went to Simbirsk, I would be deprived of all that I had been dreaming about for so long.

George had taken care of just about everything; he had gone and returned again, and the day of our departure was set for the first of June. There was nothing that could be done; I had to say goodbye to my friends, who were leaving at the end of May for Nizhny. I felt sad. The future did not seem bright.

The only consolation was that one of my favorite teachers, Anna Dmitrievna, decided to come with us. She was attractive and nice. Head over heels in love with our great charmer, George, she had resolved to take such a drastic step as moving to an unknown city where there was no prospect of employment, without having received any promise from my brother to marry her. Mother found this somewhat irresponsible; however, I was greatly impressed by her decision. With my customary ability for going to extremes, I began simply to adore her and was angry with George that he did not sufficiently value such sacrifices undertaken for his sake. He, however, was happy and accepted this as the proper expression of love due him.

The trip was pleasant. We all took our places in the freight car that George had managed to make arrangements for; and from morning to night we sat by the wide open door, admiring the Russian landscape and nature. En route, George was especially nice to Anna; my attitude changed, and I was already dreaming about the possibility of a wedding in Simbirsk, a prospect which reconciled me to this sudden move.

### SIMBIRSK

Simbirsk was spread out attractively along the shores of the Volga and was, in the fullest sense of the expression, drowned in greenery. Everything was blooming. All of us were looking with interest at the outline of the city and the surrounding villages and towns. The only person in our car who did not share the general delight was the old cook, who, having lost her position with her former "lords" in Lukoyanov, had asked Mother to take her with us—at least to help her get set up in this city, which was larger than Lukoyanov—even if she couldn't work for us. But Marfusha had not even the faintest idea of the geography of Russia. For some reason she thought that if Simbirsk was the birthplace of Lenin, then it had to be at least like Petrograd, where she had formerly lived and which she adored. Her disenchantment and bewilderment upon our arrival in Simbirsk was great. Catching sight of it from afar, she saw that there could be no comparison with Petrograd and that she would again have to vegetate, almost as if in the province she hated with her whole heart. Her observations and irritation amused us all and we carefully tried to convince her that it was much better to live in the provinces, especially along the Volga. We explained that things were more peaceful and that it was easier to get food. These explanations made no impression on her.

In Simbirsk my father's sister lived with her grandson. My uncle and my cousin, my childhood friend, had left to join the White Army. The parents of little Arsinin had also left Russia and were living abroad. The boy had been temporarily staying with his grandmother in Simbirsk, where he was stranded because of the impossibility of sending him to his parents. My aunt found us an apartment near her former house, in which she occupied two rooms, something now considered a great luxury. My mother, friendly with my aunt since youth, was especially happy about this; because, in addition to George and me, she would have a good friend close at hand.

Since we arrived in June, I was free from school work until the first of September; and I busied myself with getting to know the city and its surroundings. Simbirsk especially interested me, as it was the birthplace of one of my favorite Russian writers, Goncharov. In his novel *Obryiv (Precipice)* he had described a very beautiful place not far from the city. The view of Goncharov's precipice was the first pleasurable event of my Simbirsk epic.

At that very same time my mother more feverishly sought work and soon found a job as typist in one of the railroad establishments located on our street. My brother was travelling on official business and, being in Simbirsk, helped Anna find a new position. It was fortunate that she soon obtained work. I believe that in her case, good looks played the major role.

My life was spent in walks, giving me great pleasure, and in exhausting trips to the market with Marfusha, the remarkable cook who, unable to find another place, had settled with us. These trips soon were transformed for me into real torture. Apart from the fact that with our limited means it was extremely difficult to obtain everything that was essential, the main thing, and one that terrified me, was Marfusha's character. She hated Simbirsk, grumbled about fate that had led her so far from her beloved Petrograd, and constantly cursed without restraint and in full voice against the Soviet regime she believed to be the cause of all her misfortunes.

With George and Mother she did not let herself go too far, but my presence for some reason inspired her. I could not forbid her to conduct herself so, and involuntarily I became the quiet listener to her fierce attacks. When we went to the market, absolutely everything called forth her anger. If the coachman cracked the horse with the whip, it was the fault of the Soviet regime for permitting the mistreatment of animals. If we encountered some pitiful, homeless dogs, again it was the fault of the Soviet regime for bringing to the country such a famine. Marfusha adored animals and believed that their care was the direct responsibility of the city administration.

Other than "Herod," she had no name for those with any relationship to the city administration. To her they were all Bolsheviks, damned Communists, monsters; and she wished them all to hell. She would often stop en route to the market and begin to pour out her wrath on whomever she felt deserving. My attempts to get her to move on would have no success. Just seeing my horror, she would shout still louder, as if wishing to show her independence and bravery. As a result these trips took at least two to three hours. Even at the market she did not try to find what we needed and leave quickly, but just the opposite. She would often gather a crowd of sympathizers around her, and then she would know no bounds.

To this day I do not understand how some passing militiaman did not arrest this stormy old woman. Apparently, for the time being, they were not paying any attention to such old shouters. They had enough to do with the young and more dangerous persons.

Returning home, I implored Mother not to send me any longer to the market; however, the sly old woman assured my mother that she was unable to manage everything alone, that the city was unknown to her, and that she just absolutely had to have an assistant. It was impossible to out-argue her. Mother admonished Marfusha; and she appeared to listen, only to start everything all over again the next day.

The approaching fall and the beginning of high school saved me; our trips to the market ceased. Marfusha began to do the shopping herself, and it seemed she had calmed down somewhat. But once, nonetheless, an angry militiaman did bring her home. Not having been satisfied with her usual cursing, this time Marfusha had stopped by the house where Lenin and his family had once lived. She began to call upon the passersby to bear witness that this anti-Christ was the one guilty of the poverty in the country, people dying from hunger, typhus, and cholera. She was surrounded by people, and many sympathized with what she was saying. Thus, her thundering speech kept continuing and finally attracted the attention of a guardian of public order. Despite her opposition, he twisted her arms behind her back and led her home. Fortunately for her, the fellow turned out to be rather peaceable (or maybe he too was already fed up with the Soviet regime). At any rate, he confined himself to the remark that the landlord of our place should not let this old lady out on the street, and if it happened again she would definitely go to jail for her anti-Soviet outbursts.

For Mother this was extremely unpleasant, and at the first opportunity she placed Marfusha with a family that was leaving for Petrograd. They promised to deliver the old lady to the people for whom she had formerly worked. We sighed with relief; and although I now had to go to the market alone after school, I was happy and did so far more quickly.

The cholera epidemic began to abate toward fall, and not one of us came down with it. School now brought me many varied diversions, new acquaintances, and friends. George was constantly on the road. When he was in Simbirsk, he would visit sweet Anna; but it could already be felt that the former love between them no longer existed. Mother continued to work, and life in Simbirsk seemed to be satisfactory.

The 8th of March, the day of the Women's Holiday, it was announced in Simbirsk that every woman could receive two rubles. These could be obtained by going to the designated place in a given region. I disregarded this grandiose gift of the Soviet government and did not go. My mother went. She decided that, as the Russian saying goes, a clump of wool can be obtained even from a worthless sheep. A few hours later she returned extremely annoyed. She had had to stand in line for a very long time; and, worst of all, the old woman who was standing ahead of her in line was literally crawling with lice. At that time an epidemic of typhus was beginning in Simbirsk, and lice were the main carriers of this frightful disease.

Nine days later Mother went to bed with a high fever. The doctor diagnosed typhus. All the hospitals were overfilled and our situation became very difficult. Mother had to remain at home, and the neighbors were fearful of becoming infected and would jump away from me whenever I would go to the kitchen. As we were living in a communal apartment, it was necessary for me to go through the dining room in order to get to the corridor or to the kitchen. The former owner of this apartment, an ex-tsarist general, slept in the dining room. He would usually sit in an armchair in the middle of the room; but now he would hide behind the screen where his bed was, especially when I would appear.

I felt as though I had the plague and tried as much as possible to remain in the room I shared with Mother. This was practically impossible since something was always needed from the kitchen. Mama was delirious and kept wanting something to drink. I could not ignore her requests; and, disregarding the angry old fellow, I would rush through the dining room and corridor into the kitchen. The other residents would disappear immediately as if by the wave of a magic wand.

Mama's hair was shaved down to the skin; and she looked very thin, like a *Bezprizhorniki*. She had lost twenty pounds. The doctor came every day and, seeing my despair, would cheer me up saying that Mama had a good heart, that she was still young, and that she undoubtedly would survive such a serious illness. And indeed, the crisis passed. Mother got better; however, I became ill. This made matters worse, since now both of us required care.

My aunt, father's sister, disregarded all warnings and cared for us until Mother recovered. My illness was so strange that the doctors had to have a consultation about this type of rare typhus. Despite all symptoms of the illness I did not lose consciousness and did not become delirious, although my temperature was very high. After nine days I was already up and felt almost normal. To my great satisfaction, I had not been shaved, something I had greatly feared. I considered my long hair to be my most attractive asset.

Mother was ill for a long time and did not go to work. She was granted a sick leave. I, however, wanted to get back among acquaintances and school friends as quickly as possible. Since I felt completely restored, the doctors gave their consent and did not hold me to the quarantine.

Thus March and April slipped by, and my favorite time of the year for the Volga was approaching. In May, after the spring thaws, the flooded river presents an unforgettable spectacle. This is especially so when the first green appears in the gardens and parks of our picturesque city.

George was transferred to distant Orenburg. It made no sense to follow him there. My cousin Paul, a fourteen-year-old boy, returned from Siberia after having buried his father. Kolchak's campaign had ended in failure. In my aunt's house there was simultaneously joy and sorrow. The son had returned; the husband had not.

At this time Mama received a long letter from my father by way of Switzerland. He described in detail all that he and Paul had gone through. Having gotten through to the South, they had joined the Wrangel Army, fighting on the White side. Paul had been given the command of a company of the Daghestan Regiment, and Father had been accepted as a junior officer. The war was not ending, and the Reds were on the offensive.

The desperate battles on the Crimean isthmus cost Paul his life. He was seriously wounded in the spine, and had he remained alive he would have been a lifelong invalid. He died in horrible suffering. It had been possible to bury him with full military honors, and behind the coffin, covered with a red cape, they led Paul's horse. Further back followed the officers and horsemen, headed by the commander, Amilakhari. Father wrote of his anguish, having lost his favorite son, knowing nothing about us, and visualizing the inevitable destruction of the White Army.

Two weeks after Paul's burial, Father emigrated to Turkey with his brothers, Sergei and Nikolai, and from there had gone to Paris. Now he was living in Paris at the house of a French count who, once in the past, had gone hunting at Obrochnoye. Now, in memory of the past, he was giving asylum to refugees. With the aid of the count, de Trassi, he had been able to find us through the Swiss Red Cross.

Upon receiving this letter, we mourned for a long time. I was especially sorry for my mother, who had now lost three of her five children. For a long time I just could not believe that Paul was no more. Since I had not seen him dead, as I had Vasya, it seemed to me that he must still return.

Some time after Papa's letter, I was sitting in our room by the open windows when suddenly a large, colorful, pretty bird (a parrot) flew in from the street. This was such an unusual phenomenon that I sat there stunned, afraid to move for fear of frightening him. But the parrot did not intend to fly away and settled in with us as though at home.

There is a Russian superstition that when a bird flies in the house, it signifies the soul of a dead, close person; and he makes himself known thus. I did not doubt that my mother would be no less surprised than I by the visit of this unexpected guest and that he would not bring her any joy. But, nevertheless, I felt sorry for the parrot and could not drive him out. He began to speak rather amusingly, although he was difficult to understand. I closed the windows and went to consult the neighbors. They all came running to look and even brought a cage that someone had found. They advised me to put a notice in the paper; and, in the meantime, to keep him in the hope that the owners would answer and call for him.

Indeed, four days later a girl about eight-years-old arrived with her mother. It turned out that the girl had been inconsolable over the disappearance of her bird and was overjoyed upon reading our announcement in the paper. Her mother told us that the parrot had been living with them for several years already and there had never been an instance when he had flown out of his cage.

For some time after this I remained under the spell of that strange visitor, but eventually forgot. However, in the fall of that very same year my aunt received a letter from one of her brothers informing her of my father's death in Paris during the summer; she very superstitiously reminded me about our July guest. And it was with this second letter from abroad that all connection with our emigrant relatives ceased for a period of many years.

That year in Simbirsk has always remained in my memory because of one pleasant event. The Americans had organized help for the starving in the Volga area; and in Simbirsk there had been opened a new establishment, the American Relief Administration (ARA)? They began hiring everyone who knew English and who knew how to type. But in addition, those who had relatives abroad began to receive packages through the American mission, both of foodstuffs and of other items. We received packages from Holland. One of my mother's sisters had been married to the czarist Russian ambassador to Holland and had lived in the Hague. My uncle had long since died, but the Dutch authorities allowed the family to live in that very house where the ambassador's office had formerly been. Our relatives had also searched out Mother through the Swiss Red Cross and, having received our address, had paid some money in Holland so that we could receive a quantity of food. Having received a summons to the ARA, Mother sent me there alone, supposing that there would be one small package I could easily bring home. The American distributing the food and products questioned me through an interpreter and inquired about our material circumstances. He then supplied me with such a quantity of things that I could not have carried even half of them with me. I requested permission to leave all the things there for the time being and ran to the center of town, where there were always some beggars. I hired two beggars, promising them part of what I received.

An array of good things was in the packages prepared by the wonderful Americans: sugar, fat, coffee, flour, condensed milk, and what especially delighted me, two lengths of material for coats (for my mother and me), and material for dresses. I returned home in triumph, having generously rewarded my two companions with products they had not seen in a long time.

Simultaneously with the help to the needy population of Simbirsk, the Americans began to supply the schools. Now, instead of our dinners of herring and dried cod, there appeared powdered milk in cans, all conceivable types of canned goods, and white bread.

This same fall our school was reorganized into a teacher training college, and the studies were conducted in the evening. This gave me the opportunity to look for work. Soon, with the help of my schoolmate's father, I was hired as an office worker in the district finance office (Gubfinotdel). The pay was minimal. What I received for the first month's work I paid out for five yards of linen from which my mother made a dress. Thanks to the American aid, I became the owner of three outfits; this was considered unbelievable wealth. About that time inflation had reached great proportions. The Tartars were the largest deliverers of goods for the black market and for barter. Incidentally, my aunt had once trusted a Tartar and given him an entire box of valuables for safe-keeping, believing they were safer with him than with her. She never got them back. The Tartar said that they had been stolen from him. Perhaps it was true. Who could check? At any rate my aunt, her grandson Arsenin, and an adolescent son were left with almost nothing. It was just lucky that someone had persuaded her not to give him everything but to buy a cow. She had the cow, and her son was soon successful in securing a job as messenger at the same institution where Mother was working. At the time she was also trying very hard to get permission from the Red Cross to send her grandson to his parents in France.

That winter I was infected by little Arsenin, with whom I used to spend all my free time playing soldier, with the worst type of measles. The boy recovered quickly; at his age this illness was not considered serious. But I was already sixteen years old, and recovery was very slow and difficult; I lay in bed in an absolutely dark room for more than three weeks, since they feared for my eyes.

In the spring we received the surprising news that George had married. His wife Zoya was twenty-two and a pretty blond, judging from the photograph he sent. George promised that he and his wife would soon come to visit us.

This new situation, the marriage of my brother, pleased me very much. I awaited the arrival of his bride with impatience. Mother, however, was very skeptical: "Who is she? What's her family name? Why doesn't he write it? Where did he dig her up?" I could not understand what significance her former name had if she was now George's wife and would bear his name. Mother was annoyed with the way I had become, to use her word *Sovietized.* Indeed, in old Russia the name played a major role. It seemed entirely unacceptable that her son had married some Swallow, or Fox, or Ivanov. Mother even complained to my girlfriends, who could not understand anymore than I what difference it made. Deciding not to ask her why she was so agitated, they later pestered me to explain to them how it was that Mother, who didn't even know Zoya, was already dissatisfied with her son's choice.

That was when the first misunderstanding, caused by opposing views of reality, arose between my mother, whom I adored, and myself. She was the incarnation of the old Russia, and I was already a Soviet product.

Soon our young couple arrived. George was very happy, joking with everybody. He teased Mother, telling her that his wife's maiden name had been Myishkin, and if we remember Dostoevsky's *Idiot* this was not only a noble name but even a princely one. Zoya was amused by all this, for she knew very well that she had no relationship with princes. She was extremely attractive, elegant, and fragile; but with her lack of "high birth" and origin, Mother had to come to terms. Zoya was a daughter of an Orenburg craftsman and the janitress of the establishment where George was serving.

George was now a civilian. The war with the White Army was over and the necessity of purchasing horses for the front had ended. He was much more satisfied with his civilian status, since he was free to choose both his work and his place of residence. Zoya liked Orenburg since her people lived there; George, however, was more attracted to the Volga.

In Simbirsk he could not find suitable work and began to dream about moving to Nizhny-Novgorod, where there were greater employment possibilities. Nizhny was larger than Simbirsk and was famous for its fair, which attracted people from all the cities and places of Soviet Russia. At the fair the most animated trade took place, and all types of new institutions were being opened. Many persons were also hired by the fair committee.

Again our restless George disturbed my peace with the question of a new move. During the three years spent in Simbirsk, I had become quite accustomed to this pretty city, situated on the high right bank of the Volga. In Simbirsk there were many gardens; and the magnificent embankment of the Volga, called the Crown, was in no way less beautiful than that of Nizhny-Novgorod. There were also two theaters, in one of which I had begun to perform in a theatrical circle organized by one of my friends. This gave me great pleasure. I would usually play the roles of comical old women and gained even greater confidence, thanks to makeup and costuming, as no one in the audience could recognize me. Our performances met with great success, and the number of spectators exceeded all expectation. When the hall would ring with laughter over my comical figure, and my voice had changed to the point of being unrecognizable, I would feel myself a real actress; and I was delighted with the career I had chosen. And now suddenly all this would have to be abandoned.

Besides this, of course, there were already romances, not only with the boys at the gymnasium and the high school but also with my stage colleagues, who were a bit older and therefore more interesting to a seventeen-year-old girl. I was head over heels in love with our director, a lad of twenty-six who seemed to me to be an extremely solid, almost elderly fellow. He seemed even more so when I found out about his past and especially his stay in the White Army, with which he had left Simbirsk a few years earlier. After his return, he was surrounded by an aura of mystery; for he was being watched. As an "unreliable" element, he had to register every month at the Militia Department. All of this singled him out to ignite the curiosity of girls my age. To be the chosen one of such an unusual fellow flattered me terribly. My mother reacted very favorably to him, mainly because he had served in the White Army, where all her sympathies lay. It had been very difficult for her to reconcile herself to the fact that George had been called to the Red Army; and, although he had not been in the active fighting, nonetheless he was an enemy of his own father and brother, who were fighting for the Whites. And thus Slava, my friend, became mother's favorite—and my great love.

If George's plans would win out against my opposition, and if Mother would decide in favor of another move, I would have to separate from Slava, too. For the time being we had not come to any decision. Mother was vacillating a great deal. In Simbirsk we were both working; and I had even received my first promotion, taking on the duties of assistant to the bureau manager. I was receiving honoraria for my theatrical performances. Although not large they were very flattering for my self-esteem. Life seemd very happy to me, and the Soviet regime no bother at all.

In the meantime, seeing our cool attitude toward his plans for moving, George decided to go with Zoya to Nizhny-Novgorod to see what he could expect. And then an unexpected occurrence turned everything around.

One night I awoke because of a strange odor in our room. Awakening Mother, I went out into the corridor and saw to my horror that the entire end of it was in flames. Although the fire was still comparatively far away, smoke was already reaching our room. My first impulse (very unsuccessful, by the way) was to open the window to the street and shout for help. There were no phones in the house, and it was impossible to notify the fire department. I was just hoping that our neighbors or some chance late passersby would hear. But in my excitement, I closed neither the window nor the door to the corridor. This created a huge draft; and smoke filled our apartment, right up to our room. Mother and I seized the first things we could get our hands on and ran out into the street through the porch. George and Zoya were living at an acquaintance's and knew nothing about the fire until morning. Toward morning, however, despite the aid of the firemen, half the house had burned; and our room, although it had remained intact, was so saturated with smoke that it was necessary to throw out almost all of our belongings. It was impossible to live in such an apartment, and to find a new apartment was not easy. This occurrence was the decisive factor in our hurried move to Nizhny-Novgorod. With that superstition characteristic of Russians, we came to the conclusion that it was the will of fate.

## *NIZHNY-NOVGOROD*

The family of my grieving aunt was standing on the pier in Simbirsk. My friend Slava was also there, shocked and dismayed by my unexpected departure. The steamer had left the shore some time ago, but I was still standing on the deck and sobbing bitterly. It seemed as though life had come to an end. Nothing Zoya, Mother, or George could say had any effect. Having become convinced of the futility of their attempts to calm me and get me to go to the cabin, they apparently decided that time heals all wounds, especially the love dramas of a seventeen-year-old girl; and they left me and went to the cabin to sleep. I, however, remained on the deck until morning; and only at dawn when the curious deck scrubbers appeared, did I decide to retire and hide my flushed and swollen face.

During the three-day journey, although I continued to grieve, the original feeling of despair left me, and I began to admire the charming view of the Volga shores. Nature had always made a strong impression on me; but the Volga at the beginning of June, especially in magnificent weather, presents an unforgettable sight.

Nizhny-Novgorod was the city of my early childhood. From the first days, these youthful childhood memories took hold of me. We stopped in the old hotel where we always stayed when we happened to visit Nizhny in the past. I had stayed there with Mother in the spring of 1917 when I took the exam for the Nizhny gymnasium.

The next day I went to stroll through the city. There was the house where I was born and had lived till the age of seven—now it was ZAGS, the bureau for registering marriages of Soviet citizens. I went further; there was the building of the former institute of the Nizhny-Novgorod gentry. Here was the Nizhny Kremlin, where the family of my uncle had lived, my uncle who had served as secretary to the governor. Now the city administration was in the Kremlin.

Everything had changed, but nevertheless it was familiar.

And here was my dear Volga! The wide, beautiful Volga with its wonderful slope. I stood for a long time on the shore and could not tear myself away from the picture which presented itself to my eyes. No matter what our future might bring, it was still good to return to one's native city.

The very first evening George brought his old army friend Skrjabin, who was living in Nizhny, to our place. This was that same Skrjabin who had visited us back in Lukoyanov. He promised to help George in his search for work.

We too had to start organizing our lives. My mother and I registered at the labor bureau, without which it was impossible to get any job. George went first of all to the housing bureau, in order to be on the list for obtaining quarters. It was a fiasco. They would not even put him on the list until some member of the family had permanent employment. George was unsuccessful in his attempt to find any work for himself. The fair opened at the beginning of August, but now it was only June, the most inappropriate time to look for work. As a result of this, I was the first to find employment, and completely unexpectedly at that.

My friend from early childhood, the son of a friend of Mother's, learned of my career as an actress in Simbirsk and decided to put on a play at the peat works not far from Nizhny, where he himself lived. I agreed to participate in the performance to be presented in the workers' club. The head of the enterprise was a fat, middle-aged director who was so captivated by my acting that he wanted to make my acquaintance after the performance. He asked me what I was doing in Nizhny-Novgorod and where I had come from, and finding out that I was looking for work, he told me to come the next day to his office in the city administration of Nizhny, where he promised to introduce me to the necessary people. From that day on there began in my life the "blat" (pull) that has played a major role in the Soviet Union since the very first days of the Soviets' rise to power.

In less than three days I received a position in the Nizhny Archives Administration as an office clerk. Especially important was the fact that Mother and I were given a room in that same building where the archives were; it was true that the room was of a rather strange shape, sort of triangular; and it was in a run-down condition requiring immediate repair, but nonetheless it was a room where we would be able to settle within a few days.

While the room was being repaired, my mother was invited to visit a friend in Gorbatovka, right at the peat works where I had appeared on the stage and where I had become acquainted with the director who had played such an important part in our fate. George, however, despaired of finding anything acceptable for himself and, strongly influenced by Zoya, decided to return to Orenburg.

I was immediately caught up in the life at the new place and by a mass of new impressions. Mother had renewed her old acquaintances and ties. Indeed, she had spent the best part of her life in Nizhny, about twenty years in all.

Her old friends advised her not to seek work in Soviet establishments, where youth was preferred, but to take up sewing. Until that time she had sewn only for me; and, as I mentioned in the first part of these notes, since early childhood my wardrobe was always considered elegant and outstanding—and all made by her hands. Now there was a great shortage of good seamstresses. Women were again beginning to dress well. The time of "war communism," when the greatest luxuries were frayed military greatcoats with the obligatory fringes below and padded trousers, even for girls, had passed. Now that the Soviet regime was firmly established, the shortages of the war period were beginning to be forgotten.

Mother listened to the advice of her friends and, giving up her futile search for work, stayed in the village for the time being and waited for the completion of the repairs to our future quarters.

I was entrusted with the search for repairmen and their supervision. But I did not fulfill the expectations and hopes entrusted to me. The first worker who began to paint the room demanded his pay in advance. We had agreed that I would give him a fur collar, for no one would work for the money that was losing all its value. With complete trust I gave him the beaver collar Mother had managed not yet to trade for food. She had kept it for a rainy day. Having received this rich reward, the painter in question did not appear again. I decided not to inform Mother of this story and to correct the mistake of my inexperience. One of my new co-workers, to whom I had complained about such deceit, felt sorry for me and finished the work for free.

While the room was being repaired, I lived with a neighbor who guarded the archives. Except for the young co-worker who had helped me, all the employees there were genuine "archive rats" and appeared to me to be no less than seventy years old.

They were all very nice to me, apparently happy that a young person had appeared on their horizon, a young person who was making their breaks entertaining—and these began to drag on for a longer time than formerly. To speak frankly, there was practically no work to be done in the archives, as a rule. The director of this heaven-blessed establishment, an old former landowner named Priklonsky, who had somehow managed to gain the confidence and trust of the Niznhy-Novgorod authorities, had employed all these workers; and the authorities paid no attention to the status of the workers he chose.

When everything was finished in our apartment, I summoned my mother from the village. She arrived and found that I had fulfilled my trust splendidly, and that it was even cozy and comfortable in our new residence. For the comfort I was obliged to the director, who had allowed me to take the necessary furniture from the warehouse of the former gentry assembly. I selected several tables, two small chiffoniers, and two armchairs. Beds were received from acquaintances. What especially bothered me was the fact that all of these things, with the exception of the beds, of course, were gold and in no way harmonious with the rather humble appearance of our room. There was no other style of furniture in the storeroom. These were all remnants of former greatness.

From our room the door led to a dark corridor, along which, for some reason, piglets belonging to the watch woman neighbor were constantly running. She kept them in a closet at the opposite end of this long, dark corridor; but they often broke out of there and, oinking, came past our room walking between the legs of the young men with whom I had become acquainted during our short stay here, and who had come to visit me. The young fellows would jump aside, taking them at first for rats. Later on they became used to this strange phenomenon and continued to call for me to go to the movie, to the theater, or to a party in the neighboring university. The presence of the piglets bothered me only at first. What a person could not become accustomed to, living in our Soviet state; and anyway, piglets are better than rats. Having in mind the acquisition and raising of pigs, the concierge had gotten rid of the rats right away, in order to avoid such a cohabitation. Thank goodness that all of this took place before we came; I always experienced an unbeliev-able horror of rats. During the famine in Simbirsk they had even dared to go through the institutions, destroying paper in their search for something edible.

During this period the stone countrywoman, as my mother and I called her, made her appearance. She came the first time with a request for Mother to sew her a dress. Mother was sorry that her first client made such an unfavorable appearance. What type of dress could sit well on such a square, fat, and unattractive woman? But what could we do? We could hardly turn her down when we had no other customer. Mother set to work; and, to the amazement of everyone, the dress looked rather well on fat Agafya. Our client was in ecstasy, as she turned and twisted in front of the gilded mirror. I had requested this mirror from the director for the professional occupation of my mother. From that day on the stone countrywoman dropped in often, enamoured with the idea of marrying off both my mother and me. Why or how she ever got that idea into her head, we could not figure out. We in no way complained about our celibate situation; for, on the contrary, we were living at that time completely at ease. My mother was a bit more than fifty-years-old and was still quite attractive; however, she had given no thought to marriage. I was still so young that I had no intention of getting attached to anyone, no matter who he might be. Since we did not convince Agafya to leave us in peace, she refused to give up and, like a genuine matchmaker, would appear almost every day with a new proposal. Somewhere she had become acquainted with a widower, about fourty-five—of a poor appearance, by the way, and with a very good opinion of himself. He was a native of Nizhny from a very famous family of merchants, prior to the revolution. We too had met him on a number of occasions at the homes of mutual acquaintances; but Mother had never invited him to our place, let alone I. Therefore, we were greatly surprised when, answering a knock at the door one evening, I saw first the face of Agafya Stepanovna, and behind her the figure of the elegantly dressed Bashkirtsev, bowing nicely. At that very moment I was getting ready to go to the movie with my boss's son, a handsome student of about twenty-two; and suddenly, there was this unexpected delay. However, from Agafya's hints it was clear that she had brought him for my mother and not for me. Taking advantage of a suitable moment, I left the room. I had not been sure how Mother would react to my date and had been unable to speak with her about him. In the confusion, no one noticed my disappearance. I had to wait about ten minutes on the cold stairway for my hero, but I was determined not to go back home.

Having spent a fine evening, first at the movie and then in a little restaurant, and having flirted with some of the handsomest fellows of Nizhny, I returned home in a wonderful mood, only to be completely deflated by a torrent of abuse from my mother. It seemed that she had guessed where I had disappeared to; and she thought, first of all, that it was not at all nice to take off without saying a word when guests were present and, secondly and most important, that a charmer such as Peter Priklonsky was no partner for me. She had been informed of all the details by Agafya, who had been everywhere and had sniffed out things others would not even have dreamed. Agafya had been keeping a special watch on me.

I, of course, immediately began to hate the matchmaker and asked my mother to keep her away from our house. Having scolded me, Mother soon calmed down and with a laugh began to tell me about the evening's awkward visit, which had lasted almost until my return. This gentleman was unpleasant to her as well as to me, and she was annoyed by Agafya's brazenness in bringing him to call.

After this incident we began to receive this burdensome person very coldly. To our great delight, sensing our mood, her visits almost completely ceased, and she no longer tried to bring suitors. Nonetheless, the beginning of my relationship with Petya had been spoiled by Mother's protests. He came only a few times more after that first evening, and nothing came of our romance.

My Simbirsk friend, Slava, wrote me often; but his handwriting brought Mother and me to distraction. I had never previously—or since—seen such a disgusting, even uncouth, handwriting. I was embarrassed that someone might see the letter addressed to me. At first my mother was silent; but once she could not contain herself and said what I had thought on a number of occasions, and it had bothered me. From that time on I wanted to correspond with him no longer. I answered his letters more and more infrequently. Apparently he understood that something was happening, and he too grew silent; perhaps he thought that I had fallen in love with another. Thus my Simbirsk love, which had seemed eternal to me, ended with the passage of six months.

When on the 21st of January I arrived as usual for work at the archive office, the director asked us all to go into his study, where he informed us about Lenin's death. This news made a strong impression on many of my co-workers, for they had trusted Lenin and feared changes would be for the worse. We were all released from work and a day of mourning was proclaimed.

Spring brought us many more trials and tribulations. The former militia commander of one of the Siberian cities was appointed to replace the nice old director. The new boss, pock-marked, of huge stature and brazen appearance, like a real policeman, carried out a purge of the establishment. He collected reports from everywhere, spied on everyone, called people in for interrogation and, as a result, fired everyone—including me. His favorite expression was, "It smells here of the old regime." And so, on the basis of this old regime a pogrom took place. For me the worst of it all was that we had to vacate our room. And it was almost impossible to find another in Nizhny. The old houses were falling apart and were not being repaired; new ones were not being built. However, the population was large and kept increasing. Many people from the country were coming to work at the plants and factories, for Nizhny was an industrial city. I was running every day to the housing administration and stood in very long lines but could obtain nothing, and the menacing new director was demanding every day that we move out immediately. The situation was becoming desperate. My childhood friend, Aleksei, who had acquainted me with the director of the peat works, again came to our aid. This time it was something different. He knew a woman who had been exiled during the czarist regime, and she had spent those years of exile in Siberia at the same time and place as the newly appointed secretary of the District Executive Committee in Nizhny-Novgorod. They sent me to him.

I arrived before dawn on the designated day. The office was of course still closed, so I sat down on one of the benches along the boulevard and in great agitation began to wait for the appointed time. When at nine o'clock I was admitted to the study of Comrade Burov, my fear disappeared. He seemed to be a very simple and nice person. I told him my request, and he detained me another half hour with questions. We parted friends, and in my hands was an order that I be given living space.

On that very day there stood in the archive yard a wagon into which my young friends were loading our few belongings. The former militia commander, having taken the best quarters of the archives for his own apartment, was standing by the window with his young wife and gazing darkly at the happy group moving me to my new apartment with laughter and jokes. My mother was already on Tikhvinsky Street, where we had received two tiny rooms in which she felt happy and free from the constant supervision of the pock-marked tyrant.

How many more times after this April morning I came to Burov in the District Executive Committee office, and he never refused my requests! Thus, through him I received the temporary use of a type-writer on which I began to learn how to type. This had tremendous significance for me insofar as finding work was concerned. Through him also I received some modest but solid—although no longer gilded—furniture. The chief of the militia had taken away my chairs, chiffoniers, and mirror for his own use.

I was no longer despondent, for I now had a strong and reliable protector. All these former militia commanders were no longer any threat to me. The woman who had given me the letter of recommendation to Burov said that even in exile in 1912, then only twenty-two, he would help each and every one who needed help. All the exiles loved him, and even the czarist police were nicer to him than to the others. And he was a fierce revolutionary and a dedicated Bolshevik. But his main worth was that he was fair and just and could not stand people like the archives' new administrator, who threatened everyone and everything only in order to enrich himself at the expense of others.

The furniture in Burov's apartment in the former governor's house was the most rudimentary. His wife was a pretty and modest woman. When I arrived he called her in and said, "Look, Katya, we'll have a fine day today; a blue-eyed one has come." He thought that I would bring him luck.

Some twenty years later, as a refugee from Leningrad with two children, I came to Nizhny-Novgorod on the way to the Caucasus, to which we were evacuating. I had received a letter of recommendation from a member of the LENSOVET to the director of the Regional Executive Committee. Great was my surprise and joy when, upon entering his study, I recognized the dear face of the elderly, gray-haired fellow, the friend of my youth, Comrade Burov.

And he recognized me, in spite of the twenty years that had passed, the thinness, and the wrinkles which had been worn into my face as the result of great suffering in besieged Leningrad. But more about this later; for the time being I was still only seventeen-years-old and Burov a bit more than thirty.

We lived in Nizhny until 1925. There were many struggles and difficult moments, both for Mother and for me. But we were saved by the knowledge that when we ourselves could not cope with all the circumstances and obstacles placed in our path, I could go to the boulevard, sit on the bench, and wait until the iron doors of the courtyard of the Regional Executive Committee would open. Behind these doors was my powerful friend who was always ready to extend a helping hand.

It was difficult with work. I would just begin to work somewhere when suddenly there would be a reduction of the employees and I, as the last hired, was the first fired. I would go to the Labor Office and receive a few pennies for unemployment. I had to change positions a number of times. Fotunately, with the help of the typewriter I had received through Burov, I had learned to type well and passed the exam as a typist. Employment became easier to get.

*EDITOR'S NOTES*

1.  Bezprizhorniki were homeless children wandering over Russia at that time.
2.  Bolshevik attempts to requisition grain from the peasants brought abouthostility and open resistance in the countryside. As a result of Soviet measures, peasant opposition, and drought, agricultural production plummeted and large sections of Russia, especially in the lower Volga area, had severe famine conditions in 1921; and millions faced starvation. In this emergency, Herbert Hoover, who had directed relief operations in postwar Europe organized an American relief mission for Russia, known as the American Relief Administration (ARA). (The ARA had earlier been directing its relief efforts in Europe.) Hoover required certain promises from the Soviet leaders: that representatives of the ARA were to be given freedom of movement and the right to organize local committees free from Soviet governmental interference. The Americans promised to help all needy persons without regard to race, creed, or social status, and to refrain from interference in political activities. On July 25, 1921 the Soviets accepted Hoover's proposal. Over 6,000 feeding stations were operated by the ARA and by August, 1922 they were caring for ten and a half million persons daily. It is generally estimated that some ten million or more Soviet citizens were rescued from starvation by the work of this Hoover commission. At the time the Soviet officials were quite grateful

and signed documents of appreciation were given to Hoover. The first issue of the Soviet encyclopedia states the following: "In 1922 five million children were receiving ARA rations. In that year ARA undertook also to supply adults and a total of ten million people were receiving rations." By 1950 the Soviets had had time to rethink the Hoover mission in light of the world situation and when Volume II of the second edition of the Soviet Encyclopedia appeared they wrote: "The capitalist world tried to sue the difficulties of the USSR. Saboteurs and spies were setting fire to Soviet plants or attempting to blow them up. The ARA helped this enemy activity." Fortunately Elena Aleksandrovna was too naive at the time to realize the intentions of the Americans and was thus able to enjoy the free gifts she received.

# 3

# EARLY ADULTHOOD AND THE BEGINNING OF TERROR

*MARRIAGE*

In the Soviet Union in 1925, the New Economic Policy (NEP) established under Lenin was flourishing. Private stores were opening, craftsmen appeared: shoemakers, tailors, etc.

An absolutely unbelievable phenomenon was the private bakeries, with wonderful white bread and other products of the culinary arts to which our eyes had become completely unaccustomed. The markets were full of foodstuffs. Even various establishments for amusements and entertainments were being opened. We simply could not believe that we were living in the Soviet Union; it was as though we had returned to the past.

In the spring of 1924, Sergei Skrjabin, my brother George's friend, began to visit us often. I would go to the theater and movies with him and with my childhood friend, Aleksei, who had come to Nizhny from Gorbatovka. My mother was well-disposed toward such a triumvirate. With her old strict views, it was out of the question to leave a girl alone with a young man. Aleksei, in this case, was something like a chaperone.

Imperceptibly a year had passed since our arrival in Nizhny-Novgorod. Already, in the spring, Sergei Skrjabin had proposed to me; and in October we registered for marriage, to the great joy of my mother, who found him completely acceptable as my husband. She was impressed both by his age—he was seven years older than I—and by his solidness. My numerous romances had disturbed her, and she always found something to say against each of my dates.

We registered in that very house of Kuntsevich on Oshara where we had once lived and which, as I have already mentioned, was now ZAGS. Most amusing of all, the registration took place in my former nursery.

We were married in the evening two weeks later, in the semi-dark Tikhvin Church, behind closed doors. Among those invited were the four attendants and only the closest relatives. On my side there was Mama and Zoya. George, unfortunately, could not arrive on that day; but he promised to come in the near future. He had left Zoya with us for the time being. She occupied my room and provided company for my mother, now left alone.

Mother took the separation from me hard, even though I remained in the same city, only a few blocks from our apartment. My husband's and my apartment consisted of only one small room, and we had found that only with great difficulty. The housing problem in Nizhny had become extremely critical. Since the beginning of NEP such a great number of people had come to Nizhny that many of the new arrivals spent the night like the homeless children of the large cities: in the stations, in the parks (during warm weather), and in hastily constructed barracks on the outskirts of town.

Three months before my wedding, I started working at the fair in order to earn the barest essentials for a dowry. For my wedding I was given three days off, and the following Monday I was sitting at the typewriter in the fair office. The only difference was that in the evenings my husband came for me and accompanied me home. This was a great consolation for Mother, who had always been greatly upset if I returned from work alone.

All November and half of December we continued to work, in order to straighten up the accounts of the fair's trade. It was only after the beginning of January that I was again free and on the rolls of the labor bureau. George spent Christmas and New Year's with us. Then, taking Zoya, he returned to Orenburg.

After their departure Mama told me that all was not well with Zoya. She was not healthy; and although Zoya tried everything to hide it, my mother was certain that she had tuberculosis, a disease then prevalent in the Soviet Union. Apparently, Zoya had spent her youth in very difficult conditions. Her parents had earned little and were heavily burdened with a large family. Besides Zoya, there were still five younger brothers and sisters. Her marriage to George had pulled her out of this poverty; but her health, undermined over the years, was difficult to reestablish. I too had noticed that Zoya often coughed and that red spots had appeared on her cheeks. When I would ask, she would say that she had caught a cold on the road from Orenburg. My mother showed great sympathy and pity for this frail creature, her golden-haired daughter-in-law with the large grey eyes in the small, thin face. Zoya was quiet and tender with everyone, beginning with her adored George. She could not have aroused hostility in anyone, since she was so sweet and cordial. I loved her very much, and her illness saddened and disturbed me.

The first months of my married life were darkened by this black cloud hanging over the heads of my brother and his wife.

### THE MASQUERADE

In February the city administration put on a huge evening ball. The wives of the most important municipal administrators were supposed to sell various things—flowers, sweets, etcetera—from ten kiosks, for the benefit of the rebuilding of our city.

Since January of that year I had been attending shorthand classes. My neighbor in class was the wife of Lazar Kaganovich; Kaganovich at that time was the Director of the Nizhnygorod Trade Commission (PROMTORG). We became very good friends and helped each other master this science that offered excellent opportunities for getting various jobs.

When conversations arose about the bazaar that was being put on, Mrs. Kaganovich proposed that I be included in the number of participants and that I be entrusted with one of the kiosks. I was flattered and very satisfied. The only thing I feared was that my kiosk would earn less, and that this would be attributed to my inability to conduct such affairs. Therefore, I informed all my friends in advance that I would be selling in the kiosk at the Masquerade Ball and persuaded them all to collect their tickets. My sister-in-law, my husband's sister, made a charming outfit for me from white silk with gold oranges woven in it. When I took my place in the prettily decorated kiosk, I began to look over all the other saleswomen; and my heart sank, for I felt that I was out of my element and that the wives of such highly placed people undoubtedly would have much greater success than I. But from the very first few minutes of sales I became convinced that the old Russian proverb, "Don't have a hundred rubles but a hundred friends" was absolutely true. All those young men I used to date before my marriage, colleagues from work, fellow students, and finally Burov himself, kept filling my kiosk without stop, choosing one thing or another. Soon I forgot completely about the existence of the other kiosks and lost interest in where and how the trade was going. I saw that my cash intake was growing and was happy that my friends were supportive and were not allowing me to disgrace myself.

The results exceeded all my expectations. But it seemed to me that only Mrs. Kaganovich was happy with my success; the other ladies of the city looked at me askance. On the day following the evening which had brought me such pleasure, I felt very uncomfortable and, not knowing what was the matter, went to our family doctor. It turned out that I was expecting a child.

The end of February and all of March and April passed in constant lethargy and in feeling not quite well. In January the labor bureau had sent me to the Fish Kombinat, where I still continued to work. In addition, I took courses in stenography in the evenings. All this fatigued and irritated me, but I wanted to continue with both activities. My disposition was definitely suffering. Mother and my husband insistently tried to persuade me to give up work, at least; but I firmly stood my ground, maintaining that my income was essential for it was becoming exceedingly difficult to exist on one income in the Soviet Union.

In April we received news from George that Zoya was very ill with tuberculosis. He had taken her to Moscow to entrust her care to a professor who was famous for the cure of all types of lung illnesses. Zoya was put into a hospital. Although such a development was not unexpected, the news grieved us greatly. We knew that George could not remain in Moscow very long because of his work, and thus Zoya would be left there alone. We remembered one Moscow relative who was not working and was also alone. We phoned her that day and asked her to help George and assist Zoya. Mother also decided that after finishing several urgent assignments, she would go to Moscow and remain there as long as Zoya's condition demanded it. She did not succeed in doing this, for in two weeks a telegram arrived telling us that Zoya had died.

### SUMMER IN OBROCHNOYE

In May my husband got the idea to take my mother and me to the country, to Obrochnoye, where my nana was living in her house. I liked this prospect. The stenography courses were over for the summer, and I had had to give up my work at the Fish Kombinat. I knew that if I felt well, I could again work at the fair, which would be opening the 1st of August. In the meantime, it would be good to rest for a month.

I had thought that I would never return to Obrochnoye, and now it had turned out differently. I reacted happily to my husband's proposal, and by the beginning of June we were already in Obrochnoye.

Nana told us about the persecutions to which she had been subjected in the first years after the revolution, because she had served the landowners. They had thought that she had hidden our valuables for us, and they had carefully searched her place. Nana had taken nothing of ours for safekeeping; but they had not wanted to believe this and put her in prison, where she spent two months. Her nephew, a prominent Communist who had returned from the front, interceded for her and got her out of jail. Under the horrible conditions prevailing at that time in numerous places of confinement, she, like our George, had caught typhus and had scarcely been able to recover from it. During these years she had lost her old father and lived with her mother, occupying herself with an uncomplicated household and rather large orchard. They considered Nana a wealthy peasant, since she had a cow, a calf, and some chickens. Vasya, the nephew, was her constant protector; and she now lived peacefully, unafraid even to invite us for the summer.

I endured much sorrow during the time of our stay in my dear village. Perhaps it was not such a good idea for my husband to send me at this particular time to our native nest, with which so many memories of a happy childhood were connected, now ruined by the revolution. I wanted to walk through the park where each spot, each tree, was familiar. I sat down on the bench opposite the house and imagined that everything was as it had been in the past, that we were living in this white house with the columns, the balconies, the asphalt approach, and the flowerbeds.

But these fantasies soon gave way to reality. The house had somehow become all black; the balconies were broken in several places and had a pitiful appearance, and Mother's favorite flower bed made a depressing impression because of its neglect and the absence of the usual flowers. Only nettles and burdocks were growing, and they were growing everywhere. Nonetheless, I was drawn further. I wanted to go into the house and into my room. The Sovkhoz (State Farm) was occupying the entire house at that time. I risked asking permission to go through the house, saying who I was. The girl sitting behind the desk was very cordial to me, and we went together to look over the home of my childhood. On the floor of my room lay a pile of books. She suggested that I choose the ones I wanted. I took a few of my favorite books, and went through the other rooms, in some of which there were supplies; whereas, other rooms were completely empty. There was no trace of our former furniture. The girl explained to me that everything had been sold at auction. I recalled that one of the teachers in the village of Baev had bought Mother's sapphire brooch at an auction and brought it to us in Lukoyanov. The girl, my guide to the house which had at one time belonged to us, apparently understood my mood and did not break the silence when I, immersed in my own unhappy thoughts, did not ask any questions.

I thanked her and went walking through the park. Part of the estate, that which belonged to Grandmother, made an especially sad showing. At the place where the house had burned earlier, there grew a thick clump of weeds. Indeed, it would have been very difficult to determine where the house had stood, had I not known exactly. Soon I returned to the village and promised myself never to return to the estate and open old wounds. It was time to put an end to nostalgia and live in the present.

In July my husband came home on leave. Two weeks later we all returned together to Nizhny-Novgorod, where I was again preparing to start work at the fair on the 1st of August. They hired me, not noticing my pregnancy, I assume. This was very good, for if I worked about two months, I could count on receiving a four-month leave with paid maintenance as decreed for all expectant mothers. The birth of the child was expected in November.

Soon after my arrival home, Mother received a letter from her brother in Leningrad, who insistently asked us to move in with him, offering us two rooms in his large apartment. His daughter had just been recently married and moved, and his artist son was working in Moscow. Their rooms were subject to be occupied. Three rooms were occupied by strangers, and it was far more pleasant for him to give the two rooms to his own relatives.

The 10th of October I went on leave, and already on the 15th we were pulling into Leningrad. I remembered our arrival in St. Petersburg in 1912, when my father had been appointed to the State Duma; I so desperately had not wanted to leave our beloved Nizhny-Novgorod. But this time it was entirely different. In Nizhny we had not been able to get an apartment; we lived in rooms. A month before our trip, my husband's parents offered us the rooms of their daughter, who had moved to the Caucasus. I considered living in one apartment with my mother and my husband's parents absolutely unacceptable. All the more, since our family was soon going to be increased. This would inevitably have led to various misunderstandings and disagreements. Avoiding conversations on this subject with my mother-in-law, who wanted everybody to act in accordance with her wishes, we pointed out that my husband had a poor position—he was managing an office of one of the local establishments under the direction of an extremely unpleasant fellow—and besides, he wanted to study in the university or technicum in Leningrad. In Leningrad there were many more opportunities for this than in Nizhny.

Without any special unpleasantness, we succeeded in settling all our affairs in Nizhny and set out for Leningrad. En route we stopped from morning until evening in Moscow at my brother George's. George, having lost poor Zoya in the spring, had already remarried. Vera was a very self-assured, rather attractive and decisive person who had moved with him to Moscow, where he had received a good position. We avoided speaking about Zoya; however, the tension was difficult for everyone. This visit did not leave a happy impression.

Aunt Ludmila, Mother's sister-in-law, met us at the station in Leningrad. Uncle was not at all well, and therefore he could not come.

We were given two large, good rooms and settled into them rather comfortably. Besides my uncle and aunt, there were two other families living in this apartment. One kitchen and one bathroom was shared between ten persons, and with us it would soon be fourteen. This did not especially surprise us, for the conditions in the Soviet Union were everywhere the same: the absence of living space, the crowded conditions in communal quarters, and the various quarrels and misunderstandings resulting from the overcrowding.

And thus there was no problem with the apartment but getting a job was not that easy. We lost hope that in Leningrad there would be greater opportunities than in Nizhny, for my husband did not have any real specialty. We encountered great difficulty. The Labor Office was full of the unemployed. My uncle advised my husband to enroll in bookkeeping courses right away, rather than in the university. Accounting workers were in great demand; the courses were six months in length. The university or the technicum, however, was a long drawn-out affair.

I was receiving a very good salary, being on a pregnancy leave; and my husband was thus able to seek work without rushing. At the same time he was able to take courses. It was very fortunate that I had worked at the fair, since the pay there was very high, giving me a good income even now.

In the evening of October 25th we went for a walk on the Nevsky Prospekt, where it was always very lively. While walking, we met a young couple who greeted my husband joyfully and with great surprise. The man turned out to be an old friend with whom my husband had worked in Nizhny the first years after the revolution. They began to ask questions and, upon learning that he was seeking work, Aranovsky, an engineer, suggested that he go with him the next day to the textile factory where he, Aranovsky, was the technical director. He would set him up as an accountant; and when my husband finished his courses, he would become a bookkeeper.

We returned home full of hope. Two hours later they took me to the hospital, to the Otto Clinic on Vasilevsky Island. My husband spent the night in the reception room and at six o'clock in the morning found out that I had born a son, without complications. In a happy mood, he went home to make the announcement; and from there he went straight to the factory, to Aranovsky. The latter did not disappoint my husband. That same morning he was hired as an accountant. At twelve o'clock, in a white jacket, as was required by us, he came into my ward in order to see his son and to announce the news of his appointment.

Life in Leningrad in 1925–26 was of a peaceful nature. Thanks to NEP there was no difficulty with food; and after all the terrible years of war communism, it seemed to the inhabitants of the city that paradise on earth had come. My aunt told us about the recent years she had spent in Leningrad, having sent her children to distant villages and to her old nana. Auntie and others, all with bags, would ride out of the city seeking food in exchange for all types of domestic items. The trains moved slowly; no thought was given to heat. People hung on the platforms, stairs, and roofs, like clumps of grapes. They turned unthinkingly into beasts because of hunger. Many of them were thrown off by the stronger ones, and they flew down the slopes. Some, losing their strength, fell off by themselves; and they met a similar fate. On both sides of the rail embankment were seen unburied corpses of citizens who had undertaken such risky trips in order to save themselves, and their loved ones, from hunger. My aunt was a strong, energetic woman and did everything for her adored husband, who had become so weak that he was incapable of work. My cousins did not participate in their parents' affairs; for at first, as I have already said, they lived in the country, returning only in 1924, when they became busy with their own lives. My cousin, a nineteen-year-old girl, married against her parents' wishes a twenty-year-old boy, the son of the landlady of the house where they lived. My uncle had reconciled himself to the fact; but my aunt, to this day, has not wanted to meet her. The son, however, had performed very successfully on stage. He had chosen an acting career for himself, signed a contract with a provincial troupe and left Leningrad. These circumstances forced my aunt and uncle to invite us to come and live with them. My uncle, who loved his sister very much, had apparently hoped that she could establish an equilibrium in his family relationship. Having recovered from the famine of the last years, he had begun to work at the Alexandrinsky Theater, looked ten years younger, was courting actresses, and had all sorts of romances. My aunt, terribly jealous, was also counting on Mama's support to tame my light-headed uncle. Perhaps their hopes were realized. During the nine months of our stay in their apartment on Khersonskaya Street there were no special dramas, except for minor flareups caused by her constant jealousy. This had no effect on our lives. It seems that the greatest disturbance for everyone was caused by my son, who had gotten into the habit of shouting and awakening the whole house every night.

This last situation forced my husband and me to seek a separate apartment so as not to spoil our family relationship.

For several weeks we carefully searched everywhere for an apartment, in order to leave the Khersonskaya Street apartment as quickly as possible. It was almost impossible to find anything; and we were already losing hope when, completely unexpectedly, through a dealer, I found that on Furshtadtskaya (now Peter Lavrov) Street the former home owner was very secretly selling two large rooms for 200 rubles. My husband and I headed there, became acquainted with the old owner of the apartment, and promised to complete the deal; although such sales were completely illegal. When we returned home and told Mother about this possibility, we discovered that house number forty-two, into which we were preparing to move, had at one time belonged to my mother's parents and was sold by them to this old lady, who owned it right up to the revolution. Now, however, deprived of all means of support, she was still living in this apartment where thirty years ago my grandmother, my mother's mother, had died. All this was an absolutely unbelievable coincidence; and we, of course, decided that fate itself had sent us there. I believe that my relatives were very satisfied with this resolution, and they helped us move most willingly.

From June, 1926 we were settled in house number forty-two on Peter Lavrov Street, where we lived until the evacuation of Leningrad during World War II. In May my husband had finished his courses, passing the exams brilliantly, by the way, and received a promotion immediately; that is, he became a bookkeeper in that very same textile factory under Aranovsky's direction.

I obtained a temporary position replacing typists going on leave. The establishment where I was working was on the Nevsky Prospekt; and it was very pleasant for me to walk there along the Summer Garden, through the Martian Fields. I always recalled how it had been in childhood, walking with my nana in the Summer Garden. It is never very hot in Leningrad; June was wonderful in this year, and these walks to work gave me great pleasure. On the other hand, my mother always looked forward eagerly to my return, anxious to be relieved of my rambunctious son. She would get very tired over the course of a whole day with him.

Summer passed, autumn arrived; and my job ended. In the fall nobody wanted to go on leave, so there was no longer anyone to replace. I headed for the Labor Office and began to visit it regularly. As a rule, people of various professions would gather at the bureau in the morning and hand their documents, mostly trade union tickets, through the little window to the employee who was occupied with the requests for work. Then they would sit down on benches and wait for the window to open and their name to be called. This would mean that there was a request for your specialty. I was not the only typist there, and they called on those whose names had been on the bureau's list longest. The first two weeks I went there without any results, spending several hours at a time. But one time they called me and offered me work in the Bolshevik, a military defense plant. What could I do? Should I refuse, then again I would fall to the very end of the long line; if I agreed, it would mean riding every day, six days a week, to the distant end of Leningrad. The Bolsehvik factory—this was the former Obukhovsky—was not within the city but in the country. The streetcar from the October Station took over an hour, and for me to get to the October Station would have taken more than twenty minutes on foot; or I could ride the overcrowded streetcar with a transfer. Winter was approaching. An employee warned me that work at the plant began at eight in the morning and lasted until five. I simply did not know what to do. There was no one with whom I could consult, since everyone in line was just waiting for me to refuse in order to get my request. Everyone was tired out by the fruitless coming and going in the expectation of finally receiving some kind of employment. Being unemployed was extremely difficult; the compensation for unemployment was so low that there was no possibility of living on it, especially for those who had no other workers in the family. I had to decide right away, and I gave my consent.

I arrived home in complete despair. I knew that my mother would not be happy. She would have to care for the child from morning until night, cook for us, and do the shopping. We all talked it over until late in the evening, trying to figure out what would be the best thing to do. Perhaps I should just refuse it tomorrow after all? But the fear that if I refused they would remove my name from the list at the Labor Bureau, this eternal fear which accompanied us all our life in the Soviet Union, did its job. I did not refuse, and I went to this factory, where I worked for four years.

This was not a happy period of my life, this daily arising at five o'clock in the morning when the entire house was still asleep. At half past six I had to leave, and in Leningrad it only gets light at ten o'clock during the winter months. When I would arrive at the factory it was still completely dark. I would hang a number on the board in the passage-way—and just did not even think about being late! Exactly at eight o'clock the board was locked; and you could be sent to the director of the personnel unit, which forbode nothing good. To my good fortune, I was not late once, due to my fault, during the four years of work there. Twice the streetcars stopped because of the absence of current. Then not only I but a whole crowd of workers and employees arrived an hour late. There was no punishment for that. A friend of mine who worked in the economic branch of the factory, and who loved to sleep late, was late three times. Not only was she fired, but she had to sit in jail as an inveterate goldbrick.

I remember that the first year of my work I was sleepless. I could not fall asleep in the evenings for fear that I would be unable to awaken at five o'clock. This upset me very much. At that time it was impossible to buy an alarm clock in Leningrad, and of course there were no sleeping pills in the drugstores.

It was during this period of my life that I came in contact with the NKVD for the first time, with this fearful establishment that filled everybody with terror.

At this time, Polyakov was the commandant of the factory and commander of the guard. He was a fat, snub-nosed peasant, about thirty-five years old. As a rule he bawled out everyone, using the most vile expressions. In such circumstances, he would show a delicacy uncharacteristic for him and lead out the women, the janitress and me, from the guard quarters into the corridor where we patiently awaited the end of his outbursts that were not always limited to verbal abuse.

It was because of Polyakov, who had two passions in life—yelling at those subordinate to him and having orgies with the girls—that I was summoned to the NKVD (People's Commissariat for Internal Affairs).

Polyakov had already been commandant for several years; and everything he had done, both his unbridled cursing and his still more uncontrolled debauchery, had been ignored. Apparently his services to the party and to the motherland—he was one of the comrades in arms of the renowned Chapaev—were great. Everything went smoothly for him. The military guard under his command trembled before him; the girls also remained submissive, half out of fear and half out of love for adventure. Nonetheless, someone finally decided to put an end to this and reported him. I found out about this only after I myself was called in for interrogation by the NKVD. At first, however, I merely noticed a change both in the appearance and in the conduct of our stormy commandant. For some reason he had grown quiet and had ceased staging his daily dressing downs; he began to limit himself to insignificant utterances and those, moreover, in written form, something he had never before done. Tetya Eva, the janitress, and I shared our impressions and decided that Polyakov had become seriously ill. He began to disappear more and more frequently.

And then one day I received a note to appear at a specific time at the NKVD on Liteiny Avenue. Still not knowing the reason for this summons, I was quite uneasy; although I kept trying to calm myself with the fact that arrests did not take place among us in such a noble and liberal manner. Since the first days of the revolution, arrests had been conducted by bursting into apartments at night and dragging the unfortunate victims from their beds.

On my note was written "confidential;" this meant that I could not discuss this matter either with my coworkers or with the people at home. Just before leaving, I left a little note to my husband under the pillow. Had I not returned before night, he would find it and know why.

At the designated time I was already standing by the entrance to the building with the note in my hand. The desk officer phoned someone, and in a little while a young soldier came for me. Not speaking to me, he led me down what seemed to be endless corridors. Stopping before a door, he ordered me to sit down on the bench and wait until I was called. All my courage and assurance that they would not arrest people in this way disappeared and gradually gave way to a feeling of fear. I no longer had any hope of returning home.

The longer I sat, the greater grew my feeling of helplessness and terror of this all-powerful organ of the Soviet regime. When I was finally called into the investigator's office for questioning, I felt that the blood had drained from my face. He stared fixedly at me, snickered and said, "Well, why are you trembling like an aspen? Are you frightened? Sit down and talk, only watch out that you don't lie." From his first words I understood what it was all about. The orgies of Polyakov had become known to too wide a circle of persons, and the command had ceased to cover up his activity. The NKVD had apparently conducted an exhaustive investigation. I had been summoned as one of the witnesses. The investigator asked whom I knew of the many girls the commandant had chosen as love partners, and whether he had not invited me to participate in his orgies. He was also interested in Polyakov's general character and in various remarks made by him. I tried to answer frankly; and he, obviously not having any accusations against me, soon let me go. I sighed with relief when I was again going down the dark corridor in the company of the young NKVD man. The bright light on my face in the investigator's office had had a depressing effect. When again outside on the street, in my joy I even thanked my silent companion and rushed home almost at a run. It was still early; and Mother was surprised that I had been let go from work so early, for it was the 13th of February, the day of my birth.

Polyakov was taken away, and I never saw him again. A nice young fellow, Klyushin, a member of the party since 1918, was appointed to his position. This man conducted himself entirely differently from Polyakov. The wild shouting at subordinates was no more; the mysterious disappearances ceased, and the atmosphere of tension in which work had formerly been conducted disappeared. Much later our janitress told me that she had been called in on a number of occasions in connection with the Polyakov affair. She, being older and more experienced and having served longer under Polyakov, naturally knew far more than I. At the interrogations she had answered frankly and did not cover up the dirty activity of the commandant.

By that time my husband and I already had many acquaintances in Leningrad. In spite of the difficulties of life, we and our friends loved to entertain each other. Before I worked at the factory, we had gathered fairly often to dance. Usually these parties were arranged for the evening before the day off; back then it was still Sunday. But after I began work at the Bolshevik I had stopped being interested in these happy gatherings. I was so tired from the week of sleepless nights and long travelling to work that I preferred to get caught up on sleep, and on Saturdays I lay in bed with the joyful knowledge that on the next day I could sleep at least till nine or ten o'clock.

I remember this period for still one more measure of the Soviet regime: the "pumping out of gold." They began to arrest dentists and former merchants suspected of possessing a huge supply of gold. They would be imprisoned indiscriminately for twenty-four hours and more, depending on when they would confess and produce what was demanded. These were very special arrests; they would be put in unbelievably overheated quarters where it was very difficult to breathe. It was rare that anyone held out for more than twenty-four hours and failed to give up absolutely everything that he had succeeded, rightfully or wrongfully, in preserving.

Some, whom they suspected of not having given up everything, they put in again. Those persons who had sat in these "Turkish baths" said that it was impossible to endure this torture. There were neither beds nor chairs in the chambers; everyone had to stand. Sweat-covered, in unimaginable heat, those arrested would stand pressing one against the other, not even being able to move an arm since it was so crowded. There were no charges against them except one: the possession of gold that was supposed to have been given voluntarily to the state. I remember that during this time I stopped wearing my gold wedding ring; for the commandant of the factory (this was still during Polyakov's tenure) had remarked to me on a number of occasions that it was bourgeois prejudice to wear a wedding ring. He said that it would be much more noble to give the gold to the government where it was needed to reestablish the economy that had suffered so much from the war with the enemies of the people, the White Army. In order to protect myself, I had to deceive him by saying I had given up my ring. In actuality, of course, I had hidden it away.

We could hardly wait for our two-week vacation when all of us, Mama, my husband, our young son, and I could go to Nizhny to visit my husband's parents and show them our heir.

En route we stopped in Moscow, where we met Cousin Olga, in

whose arms my brother Paul had died in the Crimea. Olga told us how they had met and become acquainted. At that time part of the White Army had been concentrated in the Crimea, at Simferopol, where Olga, her mother, and her sister were living. Life was very difficult for the entire population. In order to make a living, my aunt had decided to open a restaurant. Her daughters helped her. Very soon all the young officers became regular customers; and they told my brother that not only could one eat well there, but one could also become acquainted with two charming girls.

Paul did not delay going there; and, while waiting for the hostesses, he started to look at the portraits on the walls. To his amazement, he saw a portrait of Mother. He had discovered the family of Mother's brother. The pretty girls were his cousins. Soon such a great love flamed up between Olga and Paul that he became her fiancé, and they began to make plans for a happy future after the end of the Civil War and the victory of the White Army over the Bolsheviks. But their dreams were not destined to be realized. In the defense of the Crimean peninsula, Paul was fatally wounded and died in her arms.

While in Moscow, we also stopped at George's place. Vera was expecting a child; and George, who had always dreamed of having children, was taking very good care of her. We spent one day in Moscow and returned to Leningrad. It was the end of July. By September we received news from George that a daughter, Elena, had been born.

We returned to work, where we learned the unpleasant news that the six-day work week had been introduced. Although the day off was now every five days, instead of the former six, my husband's day off no longer coincided with mine. The same thing happened with our friends. It became still more difficult to have parties, because one of us always had to work the next day. Our gatherings took place on the state holidays, the 1st of May, the 7th of November, and New Year's. Nobody spoke about Christmas any longer, and if a tree was put up for the children, it was carefully hidden. People were afraid of being reported for celebrating a church holiday. I remember that one year I had somehow managed to obtain a spruce tree and had put it in our bedroom behind the beds. On that very day, the woman who was the house manager needed to use the phone. Nobody in the apartment building had a phone. However, my husband, as treasurer of Zhat, had the right to a phone; and of course the house manager could use it too. I had to put Mama in bed right away, saying that she was seriously ill. And then I led the house manager through another door further from the hidden tree, which, if you can believe it, smelled intoxicatingly of needles. What tricks one had to resort to, just in order to be able to live and not be persecuted.

# 4

# THE 1930s: THE GREAT TERROR, AND THE COMING OF WORLD WAR II

In 1930 our family suffered another tragedy. George and Vera's three-year-old daughter died. Vera wrote that George was in complete despair, having lost his beloved only child. By 1933 they had left Moscow and were living in Omsk. We saw them that year when they visited us in Leningrad with their little son; George had changed greatly. We found him aged and terribly sad.

The 1930s were characterized by one additional measure of the Soviet government, the collectivization of agriculture and the introduction of ration cards for bread. Even in Leningrad where supplies had always been better than elsewhere shortages were felt first on one thing and then another. Lines appeared for all types of items that were in very short supply. Rumors about heart-rending events in the Ukraine began to circulate. Entire villages were dying out. One acquaintance, who had managed to reach Leningrad by hook or by crook, said that in the large village where she had spent her whole life virtually everyone had died, except for a few families that had managed to escape before hunger had sapped all their strength. These persons had left on foot from this once rich area, formerly nicknamed the breadbasket of Russia. Now the entire region presented the picture of a giant cemetery.

There was sufficient bread in Leningrad; however, one item after another would disappear from the stores: first it would be butter, then sugar, then cloth. One would have to stand in line for hours. Russians had become used to lines; and no one protested, knowing that protest was dangerous. Spies were everywhere. Any misplaced word could mean jail or Siberia. People were afraid to make the least criticism; and if anyone did say something, it was preferable not to answer for one could be involved in "counter-revolutionary propaganda." During the many years since the Revolution, people had become used to keeping quiet.

These lines sometimes caused comical situations. For example, some long awaited textiles would be available and you would wait in line for the fabric. You would stand for hours. When you would finally reach the desired counter, it would turn out that what you wanted was no longer there. To leave with empty hands would have been a shame. So you would order them to cut any type of cloth, not even knowing whether it could be used for anything. You never had a chance to think about it. Those behind you would say "Take what they're giving." Indeed, giving was the word used. This word "giving," as though for nothing, for many years remained part of the Soviet daily vocabulary.

On the first of December, 1934, Kirov was murdered. [1] At this time I was no longer working at Bolshevik but had obtained a position at GIPROTSVETMET (the State Institute for Projected Factories for Non-ferrous Metals). This establishment had just been organized and was located in an adjacent part of the Alexander III Museum with an exit onto the Griboedov Canal, almost next to the church "Na Krovi" ("On the Blood," referring to the murdered Alexander II).

On this memorable day there was a large meeting in our establishment; everyone, of course, was supposed to be present. They spoke about the treason of vile provocateurs, about counterrevolutionaries who were continuing everywhere to fight the Soviet regime, wherever they could worm their way in. Everybody was in a downcast mood, and all types of repressions were expected. It was hardly likely that everything could remain unchanged.

We were not deceived in our forebodings of misfortune. A few days after the murder, the Party Committee announced a purge at our institute. This purge took place in the following manner. At a general gathering of all the employees and workers, one or another colleague who was undergoing scrutiny that day would have to get up and relate his complete pedigree and history not only about himself but also about his parents, his grandfather, and grandmothers. Of course, everyone tried to represent himself as a genuine proletarian never having had any property, having studied on pennies from his working father or his charwoman mother. Sometimes everything went fine. At times, however, things happened such as an incident that took place at one of our gatherings. A young fellow was telling about his impoverished childhood when someone, apparently from that same village, asked him about the two-story brick house, the best in the village, that had belonged to his father. Stone and brick houses were a rarity in our villages and usually belonged only to the so-called Kulaks—the richer peasants. The young fellow became very confused, for he had just called that house an izba, or hut, covered with straw. He was not allowed to get out of this unpleasant situation, and the next day he was fired for lying at a Communist meeting. He himself, by the way, was a Party member, but he did not remain one for long after this event.

Several years later I met him on the street but hardly recognized him. I was afraid to ask him what had happened after that unfortunate assembly.

Purges were begun in the institutions of learning as well as in other establishments. Students whom we knew told us that it had been done in the same manner and even more solemnly than with us at the GI-PROTSVETMET. For example, a friend of mine who was studying at the First Pedagogical Institute related that they had set up something like a tribunal at their place. The person who was undergoing the interrogation would stand there in the front of the room, and he had to give a detailed account of his whole life. Again, if something did not coincide with earlier testimony or with the information of other witnesses, then he or she was purged from both the union and from the university.

I have no idea at all what saved me, but I was not called for the purge. Maybe I was such a small fry that no one reported me.

Besides the purges, mass arrests began in that terrible December. They seized almost anybody who had been suspected by the NKVD. One of the first to be arrested was our neighbor in the apartment, a fellow of twenty-seven who was serving in one of the numerous establishments that had recently been opened. He worked diligently from morning until five o'clock; and upon returning home he would prepare dinner for himself and his mother, who was not able to work. He spent all his evenings at home. We knew him as a quiet, modest young fellow, extremely devoted to his invalid mother.

Once, at two o'clock in the morning, a sharp, continuous ring was heard in our apartment. Everyone woke up with one feeling and with one question on their lips: "For whom had they come?" By then we had already heard about several arrests among our acquaintances. Fearing that perhaps they had come for my husband, I decided to go and open the door myself. Two NKVD men entered, along with our confused and frightened janitor. The later immediately indicated to them the door leading to the rooms of our neighbor, Pavlov. My heart felt lighter; at least this time it was them and not us. I was very sorry for the nice neighbors; but, nonetheless, as the old Russian proverb says, "One's own shirt is closer to one's body."

The search continued until morning. Of course no one in the apartment could sleep. We were all waiting to see how it would end. In the morning one of the searchers asked permission to use our phone, and it was after this conversation that they took Pavlov away.

The telephone, as I already mentioned, was hanging in our room. A few days before this search, frightened by the purges and arrests that were beginning to occur, I had decided to purchase a large portrait of Molotov, who was at that time Minister of Foreign Affairs, and hang it on the same wall as the telephone, among the photos of my children and family. I even bought a blue velvet frame exactly like the other ones. When my husband returned from work, he was surprised to see the portrait of his namesake (Molotov's name, as is known, was Scriabine); and he asked me what it was supposed to mean, and why I had hung this portrait among our family photos. In general, we had no portraits of the Soviet leaders, and this unexpected phenomenon surprised my husband. I told him that, in my opinion, this could provide a certain amount of protection. He was rather critical of my action, but he didn't argue.

Nonetheless, he was soon convinced that I was right. Everyone who used our telephone saw this portrait immediately. They wanted to question but did not, although they probably had doubts. Since, in most cases, it was the house manager who came to use the phone—and the house manager, of course, was the one who was supposed to report on the tenants of the house—I believe that she must have mentioned the portrait of Molotov hanging among those of the members of our family. In any case, the arrests continued. Whole trainloads of prisoners left Leningrad every day, heading east, but my husband was not bothered. He often said to me, "You know, it's even a bit awkward to meet women acquaintances whose husbands have been arrested and sent off to Siberia. What can they be thinking about me?" It seemed to him that only he remained, and that he would soon be suspected of being an informant in the service of the NKVD.

Pavlov was also sent to Kazakhstan; strangely, they let him out for a few days with the obligation to appear with his mother on a specified day. Such a case was extremely rare. We racked our brains over such a strange procedure and finally concluded that despite all intentions, the NKVD investigators could find absolutely nothing to charge him with; but, nonetheless, they considered it better to rid themselves of such elements. He was from the gentry, and that in itself was enough. We never saw either him or his mother again. She undoubtedly did not survive the conditions of the exile.

The entire spring of 1935 we lived in constant fear. My husband's best friend was arrested. He had just recently been awarded a medal of one of the highest orders for his construction of military installations near Kronstadt. He was an engineer and had no sins to atone for, except one thing, completely unacceptable in the Soviet Union; his name was

Goering! He was exiled, and shortly thereafter his wife was sent away as well. She was a young, pretty woman who was occupied only with flirting and romances and in no way with politics.

A family of Communists, a senior political worker, his wife and mother, moved into our apartment, into that half formerly occupied by Pavlov. Now we had to be very careful and not say anything that might be misconstrued. This was not easy, since there was only one common kitchen for all four families living in the apartment. I was especially afraid for my mother, who could not reconcile herself to the various laws and regulations of the Soviet state and often expressed her dissatisfaction. I implored her to be quiet, unless she wished to destroy us. She promised, but nevertheless an unpleasant story now unfolds. Mama believed that icons should be hanging everywhere in the apartment; and, not content that she had set up an entire iconostasis in her own room, she also hung one in a corner of the kitchen. The new resident immediately noticed this anti-communist measure, and summoned my husband. I could hear the agitated voice of Semenov demanding from my husband that he immediately remove these pictures, as he expressed it; and if Auntie (my mother) wished, she could hang them in our room, but not try to spoil rooms of common use: that is, the kitchen, the bathroom, and the corridor.

This was all extremely unpleasant for my husband. When this conversation with Semenov concluded, he went to Mother and spoke seriously to her. It should be noted that my husband and my mother had always had a most wonderful relationship, and that this was the very first time that I had heard such a displeased tone when speaking to her. Without even excusing himself, my husband walked out.

Now we were afraid to converse above a whisper in my room, which was adjacent to the neighboring apartment; we felt that they might be eavesdropping on us.

Once, coming home from work, I found my sister-in-law, my husband's brother's wife, at our place. Her first marriage had been to a famous Muscovite, Ryabushinsky; and, since his death, she had kept her diamonds (of a size I had never seen in my entire life) carefully hidden. She had brought them out only once to show the type of gifts she had once received. Now, however, when the wave of arrests had still not quieted down, Lyubov decided that the very best thing to do was to give these jewels for safekeeping to Mother, for whom she had complete trust and respect. Besides these huge diamonds (the size of a bird's egg), she had brought several other remarkable jewels. Mother was horrified by the sight of such wealth and implored her to take them back. For some reason Lyubov especially feared the coming night, and she insisted on leaving these things. She left, not taking her jewels with her; and, as strange as it may seem, her forebodings proved justified. That very night her husband was arrested.

Two days later, Lyubov again appeared at our place and took back all that belonged to her. I had to ask her to do this, for Mama had stopped sleeping from nervousness and was constantly walking around with the jewels, looking for safer places. I was simply afraid for Mama's health, and demanded that Lyubov find others who would agree to care for her treasures.

What she then did with her diamonds, I never really knew. Later my niece, who lived with her, said that Lyubov sewed them into her fur coat, making something like a button. It was about a month after the arrest of her husband that she too was arrested and exiled. We never saw her again. They took her in that very same fur coat. Maybe nobody ever cut it and took those buttons apart. If not, a tremendous amount of capital was lost somewhere in Siberia.

By the beginning of the summer of 1935, after thousands of arrests and exiles, everything again calmed down. The sealed trains were no longer running, the "black marias" (or black crows, as they were called) were not rushing along the streets. It seemed to me that the composition of the population of Leningrad had changed. This was especially felt in the Filarmonia, where the concerts of our famous performers of that time, such as the pianists Oborin and Sofronitsky, were usually held. My husband and I often went there, partially because he received free tickets from his factory. The workers were little interested in such entertainments and preferred the operetta or the drama in the Aleksandrinsky Theater.

That very same spring, Elena, the daughter of the composer Scriabine, dropped in with the suggestion that we rent a dacha together. Elena was married to the pianist Sofronitsky, the best performer, by the way, of the works of Scriabine. We all loved this sweet young woman and gladly agreed to her suggestion. The next day we went to look over the dacha, not far from Luga, and rented a nice little two-story house by the Rasliv station. We, my mother, husband, ten-year-old son, and I, settled downstairs; and above were the Sofronitsky couple and their son, Sasha.

That summer left me with lovely memories. In spite of all that we had experienced during the past winter, everyone in the simple village was trying to rest and forget the entire nightmare of searches and arrests. I remember that the charming Sofronitsky attracted to Rasliv many worshippers of his great talent. Somehow it became known where he was spending the summer; and every day more and more people, especially women, would appear in search of dachas. Undoubtedly such a flood of dacha clientele pleased the local landlords, but it made a very unfavorable impression on Sofronitsky's wife. We could go nowhere with him without encountering some female, young or old, who wanted at least to greet him, even if she could not talk to him. Sofronitsky himself, it seemed to me, enjoyed such admiration and had nothing against walking through the village, responding amicably to the greetings of these women.

Like all nervous people, Sofronitsky was afraid of thunderstorms; and this summer, unfortunately, there were frequent storms. He would retreat to a corner between the wall and the hutch and sit there until the storm passed. If the storm lasted a long time and the bursts of thunder continued, we would make and serve him cocoa, which he loved very much. In general, he was a very dear and interesting fellow. We would listen to stories about his musical career, his trips abroad, and where it was that he played Scriabin most often (Scriabin was not having as big a success at that time in Soviet Russia). His wife said that all sorts of things happened to him abroad. Often just before the concert he would suddenly refuse to perform, lie down in bed, and declare himself ill. Apparently it was not easy for his wife, who accompanied him abroad. Nonetheless, they made a charming couple; and we were all saddened when one fine day, annoyed by the flood of worshippers, Elena decided to leave the dacha. Taking her son with her, she departed.

Sofronitsky was greatly saddened by his wife's decision but remained alone upstairs in the dacha. Only when the July storms developed at night did he demand that one of us come upstairs to guard his sleep. Nonetheless, despite all our attempts to satisfy him, Sofronitsky did not hold out long alone; and by the end of August he moved to town. We remained there until the beginning of our son's school term the 1st of September. When we returned to Leningrad, I knew that I was expecting another child.

It was a beautiful fall. It was especially beautiful in the parks of Pavlovsk and Pushkin. I quit work at the GIPROTSVETMET, by my own volition, since that establishment had been moved to Vasilevsky Island. Riding to work was taking no less time than it had taken me to go to Bolshevik. I began working in a shop that was giving orders for work done at home. I sewed Ukrainian blouses, handkerchiefs, tablecloths that were then sold in the reopened crafts store on the Nevsky Prospekt. I liked this new occupation, all the more since I could spend more time at home and help Mother.

It seemed that everything was going along rather well and life was more or less calm. Then suddenly, like thunder out of a clear sky, we received a letter from George's wife telling us that he had been arrested.

In Omsk, where, as I mentioned previously, they had moved in 1933, George had gotten a very good job as a lawyer in one of the construction establishments. Just recently he had written that he and his wife and son would soon come to spend their vacation with us. And suddenly they were confronted with such an unexpected event. [1] Of course, we were all agitated and worried, especially Mama. What could we do in such a case? We all knew very well what this could lead to. All similar trials had been conducted behind closed doors by special "troikas," which mercilessly condemned everybody to be shot or exiled for ten to twenty years—without the right of correspondence.

Vera wrote often, but her letters did not bring any peace. Like all of us, she had no idea what the charges against George could be. She ran around to every possible place in an effort to save her husband, and as a result she lost all hope. We sent her some gold articles we still had, with the request that she exchange them at Torgsin, if they would accept them, and at least provide George with some food supplies. We knew how miserably prisoners were fed in the jails, and we feared for his health.

Thus passed several months during which, as a result of the trials of Zinoviev, Kamenev, and others, everybody was in fear for his own life and the lives of his dear ones.

In the spring Vera informed us that George had been shot.

### THE BIRTH OF A SON

The tragic news of my brother's death came at the beginning of April; and on May 13th my second son, who was named George in honor of my dead brother, was born. Joy and sorrow took their places simultaneously in our house. Mama was so inconsolable over the shooting of my brother that we were seriously worried about her. She had indeed had her share of sorrow, and then some, during these last twenty years. Only the appearance in the house of the little creature, constantly demanding attention, dispersed to some degree the gloom and sorrow to fill our lives with new cares and interests. He was a charming boy, healthy and peaceful.

In June we moved to Pushkin, where we rented an apartment near the park for the summer. We all loved this nice little town with its remarkable palaces, parks, and lakes, suffused with the poetry of the past. As I would wander through the paths of the park, or approach the Lycée building, it always seemed to me that I walked with the ghost of Pushkin, our beloved poet, who had spent his youth here.

In Pushkin we recuperated from the tension of life in Leningrad by taking care of the new member of the family, who brought us quite a bit of happiness, and by occupying ourselves with the pictures of the past so dear to everybody, especially to my mother. At home we had been afraid to say one unnecessary word, trying to give no offense in any way to that authoritative woman, Semenov's mother, who had begun to lord it over all in our communal apartment. But it should be noted that Stepanida Svanovna was rather well-disposed toward us, especially after the birth of our son George. When we baptized him at home—even the priest recommended that we not do it in church—not only did she not tell her son about it but, on the contrary, she was the only one in the apartment who helped us in every way. It turned out that she was a believer and had carefully hidden this from her son and his wife. It gave her great pleasure to be present at a christening and to arrange everything; she even got a tub somewhere. Stepanida Svanovna crossed herself fervently during the time of the service and helped the inexperienced godmother hold the child. Mother had observed all of this; because my husband and I, according to the rules of the Orthodox Church, did not have the right to be present at the christening ceremony.

In the parks of Pushkin that summer they were filming for a movie on the life of the poet. The director, noticing our son Dima, suggested that he be filmed with the group of lycéeists (students) essential for the picture. Dima ran home in indescribable delight. The fact that he would be only one of a group hardly bothered him; the main thing was that he would be involved in a film about Pushkin. Disappointment came the next day when the director found an older and more suitable boy. Dima was bitterly disappointed.

July and August passed, and again on the 1st of September we moved to our city apartment. My husband, who had suffered in the summer from the angina that reflected the condition of his heart (he had also begun to develop what would be a severe case of rheumatism), received a trip to a sanatorium in the Caucasus. I again began working in the shop, which had been closed for the summer.

Fall and winter brought nothing new. It was beginning to seem that the wave of arrests had quieted down somewhat when we once again had to live through some very unpleasant moments.

In the middle of March Mrs. Aranovsky came to us, very disturbed and excited. She told us that her husband had been arrested during the night and the apartment had been sealed; she had been permitted to live with her two sons, boys of seventeen and seven, in the vestibule and kitchen. We had never heard of such a strange arrest. Usually the family was arrested too, or they were allowed to live in their former apartment. Being moved into the dark vestibule seemed strange.

Of course, the only thing we could do in such a case was to express our sympathy and try to give her hope that all would soon be cleared up, and Ivan Petrovich would soon be released. We ourselves did not believe any of this. Aranovsky, as I have said earlier, was the director of the textile factory and an engineer by education. What was this all about? There had been no talk at the factory about sabotage! Nobody knew anything, and it was difficult to make any suppositions. My husband, Aranovsky's appointee, was also uneasy about himself, naturally, and was very sorry for this wonderful fellow and his helpless family.

Aranovsky's arrest again evoked great agitation among our acquaintances who had up to now avoided persecution by the authorities. My husband's direct superior, Levitsky, the chief bookkeeper at the plant, came to visit us. He had been a close friend of Aranovsky, a fact known by everyone in the factory. Now he had no peace, day or night. He had already been summoned to the special section of the NKVD bureau and interrogated not only about Aranovsky's past but also about all of Aranovsky's relatives. Levitsky had not the slightest knowledge of these people living in the provinces and answered rather confusedly, which evoked even more suspicion from the commander of the special section. Now he had come to consult us about remedying the situation. His wife, a gymnasium friend of Aranovsky's wife, was visiting to comfort her as much as she could. Since the apartment was apparently being watched, Levitsky was expecting to be arrested any day. They did not break off their relationship with the Aranovskys because of their deep honesty and decency.

Aranovsky's eldest son was thrown out of the technicum, and no reason was given. He tried to get some kind of work, but he was turned down everywhere when it came time to fill out the forms in which he was obliged to answer about his father. The boy was in such despair that he did not get out of bed and did not leave the house. His mother was afraid that he might commit suicide.

Meanwhile, changes were occurring in governmental circles. Yagoda, the NKVD chief, was replaced; and Ezhov was appointed to his place.

### EZHOVSHCHINA

From an acquaintance whose parents had been homeowners in old St. Petersburg we learned that Ezhov was the son of their janitor, and that even as a child he had been noted for his despicable character. He had derived pleasure from tormenting animals, and he terrorized all the children of the house. This acquaintance maintained that he had even undergone psychiatric treatment.

This man had become the "ruler of all fates," who enjoyed the unlimited confidence of Stalin. What would now happen to those elements hostile to Soviet power who had by chance remained un-touched in Leningrad? It was this period of time, from the autumn of 1937, that has gone down in history under the name "Ezhovshchina."

I came to the conclusion that I had to acquire some kind of specialty which could support the family in case of need. I went to the institute of foreign languages and applied to be admitted as a student. Upon examination of all my Simbirsk documents—I had studied there one year at the Practical Institute of People's Education, in which was also the renamed technicum—I was enrolled in the first course without any exam. This was important for me; for after such a long interval, it would have been too difficult for me to prepare for exams in all subjects, including even mathematics, physics, etc. Since September I had al-ready begun to attend the institute during the evening shift. During the day, however, I continued to work in the shop.

November approached. Everybody was looking forward to the holidays. Aranovsky's wife, having maintained control of herself in spite of all that had happened around her, had started courses in hairdressing and, completing them successfully, had obtained a posi-tion. Her son, Yuri, was finally hired as a laborer. Little Lenya was going to school. They continued to live in the vestibule and kitchen; their old rooms remained sealed. It was difficult to comprehend why they were not permitted to use them, for no one had been settled into them. But there was no one to ask about this, and there would have been no answer anyway. Packages were still being accepted for her husband; this meant that he had not yet been sent away, nor had he been shot, at least for the time being.

Right before the beginning of the Second World War, Aranovsky was freed; and he returned to Leningrad for a few days to see his family and try to find work. No one would hire him since he had received minus five—that is, he had been forbidden to live in any of the five largest cities of the Soviet Union (Leningrad, Moscow, Kiev, Kharkov, and Odessa). He was forced to go away to a small provincial city, where he had acquaintances. It was difficult to recognize Aranovsky, not so much from the physical standpoint as from the moral. Formerly he had always been energetic, happy, and cheerful, not fearing any measures of the Soviet regime. He had been a capable engineer of very proletarian origin, which always gave him certain advantages against the "class enemies." He was satisfied with his situation and never criticized the Soviet regime anywhere. Now, however, he was a pitiful fellow, fright-ened to death, fearing to utter one superfluous word, and looking fearfully around him all the time. It was simply torture to try to converse with him! Even his loved ones were unsure of how to approach him. It was difficult to imagine that arrest and exile could do this to a person. Aranovsky did not stay long in Leningrad. Having corresponded with a relative in Yaroslavl, he took leave of his family and close friends and went to them; and we never saw him again.

In the spring of 1941 Goering returned completely unexpectedly. He had hoped to find his wife, his former comfortable apartment, and his belongings. His wife, Elena, was in exile; and no one could tell him anything about her. His apartment was already taken, and all his possessions had been stolen. Like Aranovsky, he was not permitted to live in the five largest cities of the USSR: they had given him, in the expression of those times, minus five. This rule applied to all citizens returning from exile, for these citizens were held suspect by the Soviet authorities. Goering left for the provinces where one of his former friends lived, a friend on whom he felt he could rely in such difficult times.

Goering, unlike Aranovsky, told much of what he had experienced in prison and in exile. At one of the first interrogations, the investigator decided to use physical force and drew back his arm to strike him. However, Goering quickly jumped up, showed the investigator his own huge fist and warned him that he would kill the first one who laid a hand on him. Although he well knew what would happen to him later, he preferred death to being locked up in jail for no reason. Strangely, the investigator held back. This had apparently been the first such case in his experience. Goering was not touched, and just before the outbreak of war he was released. As with Aranovsky, we never met Goering again.

Many years later, I heard from his wife's brother in Belgium that after the war Goering was allowed to live in Moscow. There he learned of his wife's death, married his cousin, and even found employment in his specialty. He did not live long, however. His body, weakened by camp and jail, could not resist illness. He died from the effects of influenza; his heart failed.

On hearing this, I remembered Goering as he was when I first became acquainted with him after our move to Leningrad. One does not meet such people often. He was tall, strong, handsome, and full of life. He was always the first one invited to all our receptions and parties. Back then he had a good position and, apparently, was highly regarded. He received an award for outstanding work as a construction engineer, and no one could then have dreamed that he of all persons would suffer under the Soviet regime. In those years all of us were still too naive and we thought that if a person worked well and was highly regarded, he would not be in danger.

The situation became worse as time passed. No one ever asked anymore why this or that friend or relative had been sent to jail or to Siberia. We all knew that no reason was necessary.

The 7th of November was the greatest Soviet holiday. I went to visit a mother and son with whom I had been closely acquainted for several years. The mother opened the door. I saw immediately that she was not the same; in a whisper, and with a face transformed by fear, she told me that they had taken away her son during the night. Knowing already about everything that had been occurring, she was without hope for her son's salvation. She was all the more hopeless, as her husband and eldest son had long since emigrated to France. This was undoubtedly known to the NKVD, especially now with such a fearful figure as Ezhov heading it. There was no way I could comfort her. We carried away the books and things thrown around the floor during the search carried out by the NKVD agents. As the mother of the arrested man said, they could find nothing incriminating and took nothing; but, nonetheless, they took her son away. The searches were now being carried out simply as a matter of routine.

There were new residents in our apartment. Stepanida Ivanovna, with her son and daughter-in-law, received a new and much more spacious apartment. Again there was a change, and naturally the worst was feared. The Pavlov quarters were on the list of the Party committee, and no one except a Party worker would be assigned. Indeed, a family of five persons moved in: husband, wife, two children, and the wife's mother. The husband was a Communist with a rather prominent position. The wife was studying in the university; and the children were in the care of her mother, a small, sickly old woman who was the complete opposite of the bellicose Stepanida—toward whom we had even felt some sympathy after the baptism of our George.

We still did not know how to conduct ourselves with new residents. Again I implored Mother to be most careful and not to enter into any conversations with them. The young parents were never at home; the old woman was occupied up to her neck with the household and the children. The greatest misfortune, however, was the seven-year-old daughter, who went into other people's rooms without asking permission and, worst of all, stole things. We were afraid to complain about her. Meanwhile, every day, one or another of the residents had something missing. The old Estonian woman suffered most of all. It was her room, separated only by a simple screen from the quarters of the new residents, that was the favorite theater of activity for the young thief. The old lady complained quietly only to us. Nobody took any measures against her.

One more year passed. My greatest pleasure was my studies, which were going very well. I received such a good stipend for excellence that I was able to give up working and be a full-time student.

My husband was purged from the textile factory for not being of proletarian origin. Fortunately for him, Mrs. Kolontirskaya, the director of the entire textile plant and an influential long-time Party member, interceded for him. As a result, my husband came out ahead. Mrs. Kolontirskaya had nothing to fear; apparently her position was extremely solid.

A month after Mrs. Kolontirskaya effected my husband's transfer to the textile plant, she invited us to go to the Marinsky Theater and share her loge. During the intermission my husband went to smoke; and Kolontirskaya and I were strolling through the foyer when a man of middle age, average appearance, and height, came up to us. Kolontirskaya introduced me to him. His name, Kosygin, meant nothing to me; and since his appearance and manner were not particularly pleasant, I did not participate in their conversation. The intermission dragged on for a long time, and I hoped that my husband would hurry back and rescue me from the boring situation in which I found myself.

Unfortunately, my husband was in the smoking room one floor down and appeared only toward the very end of the intermission. When he came up to me, he asked whether I knew the man to whom I had been introduced. Since Kolontirskaya was still conversing with him, I managed to whisper quickly to my husband that he was some completely unattractive fellow and I just did not know how to free myself from them. "Be careful in your judgments," my husband said, stopping me. "You don't have the faintest idea what a fantastic career this fellow is making for himself, and just what he is likely to become." Having worked for a long time in the textile industry, my husband knew Kosygin and considered him extremely capable and intelligent, and he observed his success and quickly growing popularity. Even then he was certain that Kosygin would shortly be playing one of the major roles in the Soviet government.

His words made no special impression on me. I was absolutely indifferent to politics and to what Kosygin might become. It was entirely immaterial to me.

The Yezhov period was the most difficult period of the post-revolutionary years. Every day we would find out about some new action of the Yezhov terror. We were absolutely afraid of everyone and everything; we were afraid every single person could turn out to be an NKVD spy. For my birthday we decided to have an evening party, as we had always done, and invite our closest friends and acquaintances. Among those invited was a childhood friend of mine, Marina Tolbuzin. Since there were always more women than men, (a majority of the men in our circle were either imprisoned or exiled), I asked her whether she knew any nice or interesting man to make my party less boring for the women. She recommended one of her acquaintances, and the list of guests was drawn up. I gave the list to my uncle upon his request, and he read it very carefully right up to the end. Then he said, "Here, these two you shouldn't have invited." One of those two was Tuchkov, the one that Marina had invited. The other was a very nice, cheerful fellow whom we had met at a number of places. To my surprised question, Uncle answered, "Because of Tuchkov, all the remaining Lyceens have suffered; and the other one has informed on a number of well-known families." Considering my uncle a real panic-monger, I did not change my list.

The evening passed; no one was bored. Of course there was drinking and tongues began to loosen. There were a number of jokes that at other times might not have been told. Everything seemed so nice and happy, however, that it never occurred to me that anyone amongst us could have been an informer. It was soon after this party that a young engineer named Stankevich, extremely leftish oriented and enjoying the confidence and good-wishes of the authorities, was arrested. After that followed the arrest of a good friend of my husband. When I told this to my uncle, he said very significantly, "I told you, but you just wouldn't listen." Life became more and more full of fear.

As always, we spent the summer in a suburban dacha; and in September we returned to Leningrad.

We awakened one night to a penetrating ring, not unlike that of a few years ago when our nice, modest Pavlov disappeared forever from our lives. I had not the least doubt that they had come for my husband, despite all my clever ruses to save him. I do not remember who opened the door this time; I was too agitated by the impending arrest of my husband and remained in my room tensely listening to the steps in the corridor. My husband, pale as a sheet, stood near me no less agitated. Fortunately my mother and the children did not wake up.

The heavy steps of several men went past. Wondering what it was all about, I glanced out into the corridor. Not believing my eyes and ears, I could see that the search was taking place in the rooms of Kuryakin, the Communist and Party worker.

The search continued until morning. Again, as in the case of Pavlov, they asked permission to use our telephone and called for the necessary transport. The arrested man was taken away, and his wife Lyubov burst into our place, sobbing and pouring out her grief and anxiety. Formerly she had been aloof, feeling her supremacy, but now the situation had changed.

The superiority was now on our side. Her husband, a senior Party worker, had been arrested just like any other "enemy of the people;" and my husband, a non-Party member and one, moreover, of non-proletarian origin, remained at liberty. Apparently she too now began to suspect that we had secret ties with Moscow because of our family relationship with Molotov.

Lyubov could in no way reconcile herself to what appeared to her the unjust arrest of her husband. She quit the university, and from morning to night ran from one office to another, knocking on all doors, demanding the reason for the arrest of her husband; one who had been a Party member since the early years of the revolution and had always held responsible positions. But to her, as to all the others, no answers were given. Several times she even phoned Moscow, hoping to get at the truth. Formerly, when she had heard about the arrest of one person or another, she had been inclined to announce authoritatively, "There can be no mistakes; he was undoubtedly mixed up with something." Now the two old ladies, the former landowner and the Estonian Karolina, who had put up with Kuryakina's self-assurance and the thievery of her daughter for so long, reminded her of her words.

She answered, "You live a lot, you learn a lot," or, "From misfortune and from jail there is no escape;" indeed, this second proverb was certainly applicable to our Soviet Union. No one can be sure that he will be spared. For Lyubov Kuryakin, this disappointment in her adored Soviet regime was especialy difficult.

A short while later I was going up the stairway in our institute and was surprised by the empty space in the spot where the portrait of Ezhov had been hanging. Throughout the institute the rumor was being spread that Ezhov had been removed from his work and that Beria, a close friend of Stalin, had been appointed to his place. There was little hope that things would be better. But there was one consolation, however, and that was that at least a madman would no longer be the head of the NKVD.

With the arrival of 1939 cherished hopes for the release of loved ones, because of the change at the top, gradually disappeared. No one was released; and, on the contrary, arrests continued and the black crows kept rushing through the dark streets of nocturnal Leningrad.

Mrs. Kuryakin learned that her husband had been sent away, and with her customary energy she obtained a pass to visit him in a distant Siberian camp. Leaving her children in the care of her mother, she left in

February. Two weeks later, however, when she returned from an extremely exhausting and tortuous trip, depressed from what she had seen, her disillusionment with everything in which she had formerly believed was complete.

Unfortunately, until a person experiences something himself, sympathy and compassion are usually only superficial. With Mrs. Kuryakin, however, even superficial compassion had been lacking since, until now, she had believed the Soviet government to be invincible. For her, the only people arrested were subversives and enemies of the people who were undermining the foundations of the state. When it turned out that an enemy of the people was her own husband who, like her, had been a true supporter of the Soviet state, she would not even try to conceal her new anti-Soviet attitude.

In that same month my cousin Olga arrived from Moscow. She travelled with the family of an employee of the German consulate, where she had currently been teaching the Russian language. I was struck by her extremely elegant appearance. They stayed at the European Hotel where I, after overcoming my fear, went in order to admire her foreign wardrobe and to become acquainted with her benefactors.

This was a new world for me, full of attractions. Olga, seeing my delight, proposed bringing her friends to our place. This frightened me no end; and I implored her not to do anything of the sort, for all of my people would be terrified, knowing how dangerous it was to receive foreigners. Olga assured me that we were exaggerating everything, that she had been teaching in various embassies and consulates for several years, and that she had no fear of anyone or anything.

Her self-confidence was unfounded. A month after her visit to Leningrad, she was arrested and exiled to Siberia. Only the intercession of the secretary of the German embassy, to whom she had been giving Russian lessons, saved her from death in a Siberian camp. After the conclusion of the pact between the USSR and Germany, this secretary was able to arrange her return to Moscow, where we again met in the fall of 1940.

After Olga's arrest in March, I was sitting with my husband in our room, preparing for the regular class in political instruction. The telephone rang and an unfamiliar voice asked who was speaking and then requested my brother George to come to the phone. Surprised by this, I replied that George had never lived here and that now he was no longer alive. The unknown caller expressed his surprise and even sorrow at the death of my brother, telling me that they were together in jail in Omsk and had been great friends. He asked whether George's mother was alive and if he could speak with her. Confused by such an unexpected situation, I had not thought of asking his name.

Mama was still more agitated than I and began to ask him about George's imprisonment and how he had been condemned and if it was true that he had been shot. The stranger began to insist that George was about to be freed, that he was in no way guilty, and that he had seen him the last time only one and a half years ago.

According to this, the news we had received of my brother's death had not been true. Further, the caller told Mother that he had received our Leningrad address and phone number from George. This conversation dragged on. Mother continued to ask him about the health and emotional condition of her son. Nor did she think to ask for his name and address. Toward the end of the conversation, the unknown caller, having established the accuracy of our address, promised Mother that he would drop in within the next few days and give her more details. He never kept this promise.

The summer of 1939 flashed by, bringing nothing new into our lives. The 24th of August we heard about the pact that had been concluded between Hitlerite Germany and the Soviet Union. At least now the danger of war, which some had been speaking about incessantly, faded into the background. [2]

I continued to study diligently. This was my last year in the institute; and the state exams were supposed to take place that spring, those state exams that terrified all students. Everybody was especially afraid of political science, taught by the terror of the institute, Professor Vozhin. In that year many were deprived of their scholarships, especially those who had not done outstandingly well in political economy, the constitution of the RFSSR, and the historical foundations of Marxism-Leninism.

For the time being I was lucky and was even considered a good student by that very Vozhin. I carefully made notes of his lectures, and at home I devoted all my free time to the study of the history of the Party. I visited meetings and occupied myself with social work. I wanted to show feverish activity in order to receive the diploma that was so essential to me.

War with Finland flared up in November. [3] Until then, no one had suspected anything. Almost at once, however, lines appeared for foodstuffs; and there began to be talk about shortages first in one thing, then in something else. In order to receive butter, you had to run to get in line before three o'clock in the morning. During recent years, the food situation had been more or less stabilized. Now, however, the obtaining of food was again irregular. A full blackout was in effect in the city. Many provided themselves with little flashlights in the form of a button, which they then fastened to their coats.

The sound of firing from long-range artillery could often be heard. The dark November sky was illuminated with rockets.

There were no day shifts at the institute. We had to go to the institute in the evening in complete darkness, almost by groping our way; and we had to be very careful. For the most part we had to watch out for little hooligans, who, like rats, were swarming around the streets, trying to take something from the few passersby. I stopped taking my purse with me and carried only my textbooks in my portfolio. All the windows of the institute were sealed tight with blue paper. They began to cut down on the use of electricity; and, therefore, only small wattage bulbs burned in the classes and in the corridors, making it difficult to study. We all endured these deprivations and inconveniences submissively, in the hope that the war would soon end. It was an extremely tense time. No one celebrated the New Year.

Once, at the beginning of January when I was again studying alone in my room, the phone rang. This time an unfamiliar voice asked for my husband, who had not yet returned from work. After my answer this unknown person, not giving his name, said that he would phone again later that evening. The unfamiliar, dull voice vaguely reminded me of that one which exactly one year ago had upset Mother and us with his tales about his friendship with my brother.

I hung up the phone with a heavy and unpleasant feeling. Who could be calling, not giving his name or leaving any kind of message, except that he would call again later that evening? My husband came home an hour after the suspicious phone call. When I told him about the call, it seemed to me that his face changed. However, he answered nonchalantly that this was most likely someone from Zhakt and that these people never felt it necessary to leave their names the way they should.

I felt that he was only trying to calm me, and that he himself seemed to be no less upset than I. A half hour later the phone rang. But this time my husband himself answered. I listened to his one-syllable answers and observed his paling face. The conversation did not last more than five minutes. He wrote something down and, seeing my uncomprehending look, said, "I already told you that this is Zhakt calling in connection with a meeting which has been set for tomorrow. The militia has made out a warrant about the poor blackout of our building."

There was nothing I could do but believe his explanation. Since that day, a fearful threat seemed to be hanging over us. My husband semed to be expecting something. The telephone calls began to be repeated regularly. I already knew this unpleasant voice very well. I never asked his name but only repeated to my husband what the stranger had said. Usually it was the same, that he would call again at such and such a time. I tried to avoid speaking about this subject with my husband and never questioned him, since he would always reply that it was nothing.

We had become accustomed to my husband's late return from work and were not uneasy, especially at the beginning of each year when they were undergoing the annual audit; but it was now already spring. All the accounts had long since been completed, and the delays at work continued—usually the days after the telephone calls from that nameless person. I endured this patiently, but finally I could hold out no longer. Once, when my husband arrived home especially late and in a highly nervous state, looking very ill and tired, I begged him to share with me the reason for his depression and bad mood.

After this conversation with him, I was told what I had secretly guessed. The NKVD had latched on to my husband in order to make an informer out of him. He had tried to prove to the investigator his ineptitude for such activity, basing it on both his lack of a wide circle of acquaintances and his incredibly heavy work load. But they would not leave him in peace until the beginning of World War II, when they apparently were occupied with more important concerns. No matter how paradoxical this might sound, my husband and I sighed with relief for the first time since this long period of suffering. For us the war seemed a lesser evil than the NKVD.

Only in March 1940 did this shameful war with Finland end. Finland had fought fiercely during those months, destroying all routes for the Soviet fighters. Mines had been laid everywhere, even in children's beds and in the form of sleeping children. The Red soldiers entering Finnish houses in an occupied village did not know from where to expect danger. The villages were usually empty but an old fellow at a stove, a child in a cradle, or a boy in a tree could represent a danger that might have fatal consequences. Everybody from big to small had fought for their little country with every possible means at their disposal. What the soldiers returning home from the war weren't able to tell us.

My husband's brother, one of the many released before the war, was called to the Red Army and spent the entire campaign in Finland. The commanding officers, of whom he was one, were issued special bright, short fur coats to distinguish them from the Red soldiers. From the trees, from the roofs, and other heights, the Finnish snipers aimed right at the commanding officers and, being good shots, killed many of them that way, the Soviet Union's position was not too favorable, and our government very willingly agreed to the proposed armistice; they did not wish to further sacrifice the military that had already suffered so heavily from the 1937 trials of Tuchachevskoy and of the Red Army commanders.

For the population, the end of the war was a great relief. Lights began to glow everywhere, and the city came to life. The food situation improved. A temporary calm reigned among us, whereas the whole west was gripped by the growing conflagration of World War II.

We learned of the capitulation of Paris and about the triumphal wars of Hitler; however, we were not worried about ourselves, since we knew about the friendship between our states and firmly believed that this friendship would remain untouched.

In May I passed my exams with distinction. I did so well in political science that it evoked the special approval of Vozhin, who held me up as an example to the others. Because of this circumstance, I almost had a complete break with my only male classmate, Miloradovich, who thought that only a man could really know about politics and that under no circumstances could a woman get first place. The mark I received, "excellent on excellent," reduced my colleague to utter irritation, and for several days he did not even wish to speak with me. This was very unpleasant for me, since I in no way wished to stand out or to call forth envy. The first year of my entry into the institute, he had helped me skip the first courses so that I would not lose so much time. For I was already past thirty, and I was trying to get on my feet as quickly as possible. I had been assigned to him as a "general load," and he willingly allotted several hours a week to work with me on all subjects, especially political science in which he was extremely strong. Now this business with the exams put him in a subordinate position, and he was seriously hurt. Although I succeeded in smoothing over the situation to some degree, a final peace with him was established only after the beginning of war with Germany in 1941. We were of the same political conviction, and both of us were hoping at the time that the war would free us from the years-long reign of terror.

After exams were finished in June we went to the dacha in Kirpichny Zavod, where the textile plant had rented an entire building for its workers. That summer we became very close to Kholmyansky, the technical director (whom I have told about in my book *Siege and Survival*). At that time no one had yet foreseen what would happen in a year, and we amicably and happily spent the summer in pleasant company and in a beautiful place. That year there was an unbelievable quantity of mushrooms, and we went almost daily to the forest with everyone in the building. We went in high boots and workers' overalls, since there were swamps all around. The general favorites were my little son George and Dodik Kholmyansky, a handsome student of twenty years. I even teased my mother who was now past seventy, saying that Dodik was her last love. Incidentally, she didn't even deny that, and later, when during the war this charming young boy and his entire unit were surrounded (which for him as a Jew meant death), Mother suffered greatly for him.

I was very friendly with Mrs. Kholmyanskaya, a pretty, happy, forty-year-old woman. At the end of August my husband, our elder son Dima, and I went for a week to Moscow to visit Mrs. Sofronitsky. She was living permanently in Moscow with her charming three-year-old daughter Roksana; her husband, the famous pianist Sofronitsky, about whom I have already spoken, had his apartment in Leningrad with his son. The couple was not divorced but lived separately, visiting one another frequently.

This year we wanted to explore the famous Moscow fair about which there was so much talk, and to get acquainted for the first time with the Moscow metro. Both made a great impression on us. It was impossible to really take in the fair in the course of one day, and we went every day, delighted by the wonderful equipment of the pavilions and the abundance of all types of things and products to which our eyes had become unaccustomed. Obviously here, as everywhere, there was the famous "show" to impress foreigners visiting the fair.

Once I went alone to walk the streets of Moscow. Coming out into Nikitskaya Street, which was swarming with people, I heard a penetrating police whistle; and in an instant the noisy street was deserted. Still not understanding what it was all about, I continued to walk along the sidewalk, when a militiaman came dashing up to me, seized me roughly by the arm, and shoved me into some sort of gateway. There were several people standing there already, pedestrians like me. Not understanding anything, I asked whether there was war again. A fellow standing near me quietly indicated a row of cars rushing along the street. There were six limousines, all black and completely identical. Not being from Moscow and having come across such a situation for the first time, I asked my neighbor for an explanation. Looking all around with great care, he whispered to me that Stalin was riding in one of those cars; and when he rode along the streets of Moscow, not only the streets but even the sidewalks had to be free of people.

During this stay we also visited my cousin Olga, who had returned from Siberia. She told us all conceivable types of stories about her experiences in jail and exile. Fortunately for her, her friend and student, Mr. von Walther, was so influential and energetic that he was able to get her out of hell.

In the difficult camp conditions one circumstance had helped her, up to a certain point: she was a most capable story-teller. This was discovered by chance by the murderesses, thieves, and prostitutes who surrounded her. At first they were hostile to this pretty, young, and elegantly dressed woman. Thanks to her connections with foreigners, Olga stood out because of the clothes that had been brought to her by her students from abroad. Olga had lost all hope of remaining alive under those fearful conditions of exile. But once one of the most desperate prisoners, who had bothered Olga at every turn, asked whether Olga could tell something about her life in order to shorten the long winter evening. It was a complete success. All of these coarse, dirty women, exhausted by heavy labor, listened to the stories from another, unfamiliar world. Olga told them and retold them all, not only about her own life but about the lives of friends and acquaintances; and also bits from the works of famous authors. The attitude toward her from all of this low-down society—in this place there were only a few sentenced according to Article 58 (for political prisoners), the rest were really a criminal element—changed one hundred percent. The women began to help her in any way they could during the course of the day; and in the evenings they surrounded her in the semi-dark barracks and eagerly listened until the hour of curfew when the guards burst into the quarters with shouts and threats, demanding complete silence.

Olga feared only one thing: that her supply of stories would dry up. In that event she could expect no mercy from the horde. Soon she began to receive packets sent by her friends, along with extra cigarettes and other rare items. These supplemented her stories and supported her authority among the exiles. Thus she survived that year and returned to Moscow where, through the efforts of her friend, an apartment had been prepared for her.

I became acquainted with this friend of hers, the former secretary of the German embassy, twenty-three years later in Bonn. I had found out about him through Harrison E. Salisbury's book *Nine Hundred Days,* about the blockade of Leningrad. Since this former secretary of the German embassy was appointed after the war to be the new German ambassador to the Soviet Union, Mr. Salisbury, in working on his book about the blockade, became acquainted with him and mentioned this in his work. Corresponding with Mr. Salisbury, I found out about whom he was writing, and being in Germany in 1965, I met with Mr. von Walther. He told me that Olga's first action in Moscow, upon her return from exile, was to go to the hairdresser. She did not want to show herself to her rescuer looking the way she did when she returned from the camps.

At the beginning of September we were in Leningrad. Those who finished the institute and the universities in the spring were sent away for various jobs, in some cases even to Siberia. All our class was summoned to the Pedagogical Institute, and I also received an assignment to go to Ufa near Western Siberia. At first I was utterly crushed and lost. It was difficult to object; I had been receiving a stipend for all those years, and those who received stipends had to repay this governmental aid and take any appointment. What was to be done? My husband was working in Leningrad, and there could be no possibility of his moving to the provinces. At this time in the Soviet Union, changing your place of employment because of your own wish was not possible. The children, Mother, everyone was in Leningrad; and I would have to go into the unknown and live apart from my loved ones. I racked my brain trying to figure out how to get out of this situation. Again Kolontirskaya rescued me. My husband told her about the catastrophe which was facing us and she offered to enroll me in the textile plant, giving me a "request" which I could show the commission. Her name had a magical effect. I do not know what she wrote there, in the closed envelope that I handed over. But on that day I was released from my Siberian appointment, to the great envy of my colleagues, some of whom had to go to the most distant cities and places of Siberia.

Later on it turned out that fate had smiled on many of them, for because they were so far away they missed being in the blockade of Leningrad. They did not have to endure the starvation which fell to the lot of our people; and many of them were able to get their families beyond the Urals, thanks to which they were all saved. This could have happened to me and my loved ones. The only difference is that I would have remained to this day a citizen of the USSR and would never have known *freedom*, which is the most important and best thing in the life of any person.

In May, my husband received an appointment to Narva in Latvia, which had been occupied by the Soviets. All of us were awaiting the resolution of this question with joy and hope of going abroad. During the week prior to June 22, 1941 our passes were given to the authorities, and our departure was only a question of days. Fate ruled differently. The war with Germany transformed our entire life. This has already been told in my book *Siege and Survival.*

*EDITOR'S NOTES*

1.  The murder in 1934 of the Leningrad Party leader, Kirov, touched off a succession of purges and waves of arrests—the likes of which had never been seen in any European state. There had been varying degrees of terror, especially against the former upper and middle classes all during the Communist period. At certain times, as in the campaigns against the Kulaks, the supposedly wealthy peasants who were not in favor of collectivization, the terror was very severe indeed. Solzhenitsyn in *The Gulag Archipelago* shows how the terror had never really disappeared. Nonetheless, it had abated considerably by 1933. The appointment in 1937 of Yezhov to replace Yagoda as head of the secret police did not mean that the wave of terror had run its course as many had hoped. Indeed, it brought in the very worst period of terror, a period that is now known as the "Yezhovshchina," the Yezhov terror of 1937-38, shortly after which he was replaced by Lavrenti Beria as head of the NKVD (People's Commissariat for Internal Affairs, a euphemism for secret police). It is interesting to note that all these three heads of the secret police, Jagoda, Yezhov, and Beria, were themselves subsequently executed, falling victim to the apparatus they had helped refine.

2.  Shortly after the 1939 German occupation of Bohemia, the Czech part of Czechoslovakia, the Nazis began to demand the return to Germany of the free city of Danzig and the so-called Polish Corridor. The Poles refused to cede territory to Germany. England and France gave assurances that they would defend Poland in the event the Nazis used force to achieve their goals. Throughout July and August there was every indication that the Germans were preparing for a military solution. In late August of 1939, as war clouds were darkening over Europe, the world was astounded by the news that Hitlerite Germany and Stalin's Russia had signed a nonaggression pact. This was all the more remarkable since throughout the 1930s none had railed more against the Bolshevik menace than had the Nazis. Similarly, none had been more savage in their denunciation of the Nazi beasts than had the Soviets. Thus the Nazi-Soviet accord took the diplomatic world and the average Soviet citizen by surprise. While the average Soviet did not quite believe that this was a true and lasting peace with Germany, most shared Elena's observation that "at least now the danger of war . . . faded into the background." Germany, however, freed of the danger of Soviet intervention felt it could safely ignore the West's guarantees to Poland and on September 1, 1939 invaded Poland, thereby unleashing World War II.

3.  Since the signing of the Nazi-Soviet nonaggression pact of 1939, the Nazis had gone from success to success. In 1939 they had occupied most of Poland. In the spring of 1940 they had occupied Denmark, Norway, Holland, Belgium, and France. Stalin felt uneasy and decided he would like to annex those Baltic territories which had formerly been part of the Russian Empire. Lithuania, Estonia, and Latvia acquiesced to the Soviet demand for bases and shortly thereafter were accepted into the Soviet Union. Finland did not accede to Soviet requests for bases and in November, 1940 the Red Army began its invasion of Finland. However, the Finns were well-led and defended their country with stubborn determina-

tion. The rough terrain, frigid weather, and tenacity of the Finnish soldiers, greatly hampered Soviet operations. As a result, the Red Army suffered great losses and bogged down throughout December and January. Finally, Soviet numerical superiority and military hardware began to wear down the Finns who, in March of 1941, accepted Soviet peace terms. These terms included the cessation of territories, including Finland's second city Vipuri, to the USSR. However, Finland's independence had been maintained.

# 5

# WORLD WAR II

The war with Germany caught us, as it did most of our friends, completely by surprise. Nobody had even imagined such a possibility, and we had been happily preparing for our move to Narva, where my husband had received an appointment. Sunday the 22nd of June was a magnificent sunny day, and Dima had gone with his school friend Serge to Peterhof, where the fountains were to be turned on for the afternoon. I was hurrying to finish some typing so I could go with my friend Irina to Pushkin, to visit an acquaintance ill with tuberculosis. At nine o'clock in the morning my husband phoned from work (at that time there was a six-day work week in the Soviet Union, and the day off frequently did not come on Sunday). Without explaining why, he insisted that we remain at home and not leave the house that day. His voice was anxious and had no trace of his usual calm. Dima had already left and I again took up my work. However, my mood had changed and the beautiful summer day no longer cheered me.

At twelve o'clock foreign minister Molotov spoke on the radio. With a crackling voice he spoke about war with Germany and about the bombing of a whole series of our cities. Three hours earlier the calm city had been transformed beyond recognition. People were running around the streets in confusion, filling the stores and the banks, afraid to be left without food and money.

That day marked the beginning of the most frightful period in the history of Leningrad—it would be subjected to encirclement by German forces, bombing, shelling, and even more deadly, starvation and hunger —a hunger that cannot be compared to anything and from which about 1 million persons perished. For nine hundred days the city underwent a blockade. Our family endured the first, and the most cruel, winter of this blockade (these eight months I have described in my diary which has been reissued by Transaction, Inc., under the title *Siege and Survival*).

But during the first two months of the blockade, July and August, the Leningraders were not yet experiencing all the horrors of war. There were no aerial bombardments. The radio continually broadcast a report that Leningrad was so well defended not one hostile airplane could get through to the city. There were daily repetitions broadcasted to inform us of about the huge food supplies that could feed the three million inhabitants for ten years. We tried not to believe the rumors about impending hunger, about the destruction of our beloved city and its population.

With the coming of September things had completely changed. On the 23rd of August the last train of evacuees had left the city. Those who had vacillated between leaving and sitting out the war in Leningrad were in the trap. The Germans had surrounded the city in a solid vise and began to bombard it, shelling daily with long-range artillery. Hunger began to be felt, especially after the destruction of the Badaevsky warehouses where the food supplies, intended to last for years, had been stored.

The Leningraders began to receive 250 grams (about half a pound) of bread daily. Later it was reduced to only 125 grams (about a quarter of a pound) of a heavy, moistened bread completely lacking in any nourishing substances. There was no longer an attempt to hide what was happening. In October, November, and December about 3,000 persons died each day. Winter came early; snow fell at the beginning of November and when walking along the street, one constantly came across corpses of those inhabitants who had perished from the hunger. Everyday we lost from illness some close friend or acquaintance, someone who would lie down and never get up again. This illness, completely unknown to us formerly, was called dystrophy. A person would swell up, lose his last strength, react apathetically to everything around him (without even trying to take shelter from bombings), and would gradually die.

In the building in which we lived, distrophies, as they were called, were lying in almost every apartment. I still, somehow or other, kept my energy and even undertook long trips to the rural areas surrounding Leningrad. There I would exchange possessions for potatoes and milk. With this I was able, with difficulty, to sustain the family. It was already impossible to buy anything whatsoever in the stores. Those commercial stores that had been opened in July, where it had been possible to purchase some items for enormous prices, had been closed by 1 September.

I did not want to lose track of my friends and acquaintances, and I still had strength to visit them. By this time no one was bothering to lock doors. You could simply walk right in off the street into a cold, empty room and find the person you were seeking, lying on the bed already virtually a corpse.

I still remember especially clearly two of these trips. I visited a friend whom I had only recently met on the street. Her door, contrary to her custom, was locked. I rang. Her sister opened the door and looked at me very strangely. It seemed to me she was not normal. She led me into the living room and there on the table were two coffins—that of my friend and of her younger sister. A few days later I went to visit a young, vivacious, successful actress of the children's theater. I had been with her at a spa just before the war, and we had spent the time very companionably. Her doors were wide open; I walked for a long time down the dark corridor, bumping into various objects, fearing to bump against a corpse. Finally, I came to my friend's room. It is difficult to convey with words my feelings and impressions when I, already inured to the war, saw a nondescript silhouette lying on the bed instead of the pretty, young woman. Moving closer, I recognized the familiar traits of her pale, thin face. She was lying on the bed, without even the strength to extend her emaciated hand toward me, and was wrapped up in a shawl and blanket; the cold was almost as intense here as on the street.

Somewhat different was my visit to two doctors, whom I had regarded as close friends. This visit left a deep scar in my memory.

My friend Zhenya, whose husband was very ill, was ready to grasp at any straw in order to save him. They had been married only a year. Our doctor friends lived and worked in the Michailovskii Palace, newly remodeled into a huge hospital. Knowing that the doctors of this hospital received much more food than anyone else, we had placed our hopes on their aid. This military hospital, which at one time had been a magnificant palace, was unrecognizable. We had to go past a number of rooms where the wounded were lying in semi-darkness. There was no electricity at all. Moans and pleas were coming from all directions. We finally passed the first dark part of the building and were overjoyed when we came out onto the stairway leading to the doctors' apartment. Our joy was premature. The entire stairway was an ice mountain, for shortly before our arrival all of the water pipes had burst; and because of the frightful cold everything had frozen. We stopped for a minute not knowing what to do, but almost immediately we decided to continue. We stubbornly fought our way up. With slipping feet, we would fall and again climb up moving ever higher. The hope of receiving something from our friends, something to sustain our lives and that of our dear ones, drove us forward. What a cruel disappointment awaited us!

Entering the apartment, we could not help noticing that there were tempting food products that had long been unattainable; products such as black caviar, butter, cheese, and, most important for all Leningraders, a large loaf of bread! Our doctors, knowing how difficult it was for anyone to get through to them, and not expecting guests, had not even hidden their wealth. They offered us nothing and did not even respond to our requests. Disappointed and disillusioned we slid down the icy mountain. After this unsuccessful visit, I no longer had any intention of making similar requests of anyone.

December and January were bad months for our family. Dima lost all his strength and stopped going to the cellar during enemy air raids. Apathy took complete possession of him. Thin and always chilled, he wouldn't move away from the iron stove that managed to give out a little bit of heat with the fragments of wood from our chopped up furniture.

Yuri, my younger son, became covered with boils; some would burst and others would appear. He, like Dima, began to cling to the stove and I began to notice signs of apathy on his formerly, always happy face.

In January there were three corpses lying in our apartment; two were neighbors, and the other was my uncle who had moved in with us during the summer. He had considered our place safer in case of bombardment, because we were far from any plants and factories which might serve as a target for enemy planes.

All of our outside windows were knocked out during an air raid at the beginning of December. Our apartment thus became very cold, almost like outdoors. It was impossible to obtain glass, and the windows were covered with plywood. The two corpses of our neighbors lay in the apartment for more than a week; because of the cold the bodies had not decomposed. Finally the building superintendent was able to find relatives who came with a child's sled and took the deceased to the cemetery. Two energetic women, my aunt and cousin, were able somehow to get a coffin made of boards and by themselves took my uncle away.

Finally, on the 6th of February my husband was able to get us assigned as staff to a hospital which was being evacuated from Leningrad. My husband had been called up during the first days of the war and was serving on the staff managing transportation for the military hospitals.

Our evacuation documents were for Piatigorsk in the northern Caucasus. Dima was brought from the hospital the eve before our departure, where he had been admitted on 6 January. He had not recovered and my husband and a Red Army soldier had had to carry him into our apartment. Nonetheless, all the doctors considered that it was better to take him out of Leningrad; even in the hospital he would undoubtedly die.

It is painful to recall our trip across Lake Ladoga, under German air attack, in a car that was constantly breaking down. We had been put into that car by the hospital authorities who had selected the best cars for their own people.

Nonetheless, we were able to get to the other side of the lake where, after a lengthy battle, one road had been freed from the Germans. This road led to the Urals and we were supposed to transfer somewhere en route. Dima was so weak, however, that we had to leave him in a field hospital. Mother, Yuri's elderly nurse, and I, had to continue the trip in a freight car along with all the other refugees. There was no place to stop and no other transportation was expected.

Our trip lasted three months, with the first stop in Cherepovets, where my mother died as a result of hunger. By chance at this station, and with the assistance of a Red Army soldier, I found my son Dima who was on a hospital train at this same station. En route we left our elderly nurse in her native village and later stopped in Gorky to wait for transportation to the Caucacus. All of this, including the miraculous reunion with Dima, I have described in detail in my diary of the siege.

My two sons and I arrived in Piatigorsk during the first days of May. There we were warmly received by my husband's relatives.

Life in Piatigorsk was almost normal, as in peacetime. The war was somewhere far away. After the horrible winter in Leningrad and the long difficult trip through Russia, worn out by hunger and war, we were now in this charming vacation city. Moreover, it was spring when everything was blossoming and fragrant. We also experienced no hunger, for there were special stores and cafeterias for the Leningraders, of whom there were quite a few. There were also open, free markets, with all types of foods; but at very high prices.

We spent three months and five days in such relatively good conditions. I say relatively, because the situation with living quarters was very difficult and we had to live behind screens in the general dining room. In spite of this, these three months left a very favorable impression. Our bodies quickly recovered; and, after everything we had endured, we greatly appreciated what we now had. Our morale also improved greatly, especially after we were able to establish correspondence with my husband who had remained in Leningrad. He soothed us by assuring that with the coming of summer, life would become much better. One could eat leaves from the trees, grasses, and even plant little gardens. My husband had planted a garden in our empty garage; indeed, in the Soviet Union, private cars were virtually unknown, and the garage floor was unpaved. In the meantime, my niece Tanya had also joined me and my sister-in-law.

Everything changed again on the 8th of August. On that day the Germans took Piatigorsk. Since the Soviet radio had tried to keep silent about the rapid advance of the Germans, we knew nothing definite about the military situation and were only annoyed and upset by the flight of the city's rulers. We had tried to calm ourselves, regarding this as unfounded panic. There had not been any evacuation of the population, but the powers that be took flight. No assistance in evacuation was given to the population.

And thus the German occupation began. This was difficult for the population of Piatigorsk, especially those who had been evacuated from Leningrad. The Germans did not issue ration cards. The local people had their little gardens and fruit trees and managed better. All of the new arrivals, however, were in an extremely unenviable situation, to some degree comparable with Leningrad.

The idea of opening a cafe-restaurant saved our family from a repetition of that hunger we feared so much. We obtained a place for our restaurant, furnished it somehow, and with combined efforts prepared all types of culinary products for our opening day. Everything we had prepared was sold out by noon. Success raised our spirits, and from the beginning of September until the end of December we knew no need. We worked a lot but felt good, because we were able to help other Piatigorsk friends by giving them work in our establishment.

The end of December and the German retreat brought a new and terrible danger for us. The Soviets, before their departure, had issued an order that all men between the ages of sixteen and fifty-five who remained behind under the German occupation would be shot on sight upon the return of the Soviet forces.

Dima was only fifteen years old, but who would stop to check his papers? He was tall and could easily pass for a seventeen-year-old. My sister-in-law's husband was fifty-five. We decided to do everything possible to leave Piatigorsk and lose ourselves in the Ukraine. Another matter that pushed us was the fact that the daughter of my husband's sister was half-Jewish. The Germans might, during the last days of their rule in the Caucacus, persecute and deport children of mixed marriages. Until this time only persons who were completely Jewish had been deported; persons of mixed marriages and the children of such marriages had not yet been subjected to deportation.

By purest chance we were able to leave with the last German detachment, a unit which was commanded by an airman who had been a frequent visitor to our restaurant.

This air force officer, with whose aid we were able to leave Piatigorsk, sent us on ahead with the soldiers of his unit, while he almost fell into the hands of the rapidly advancing Red Army. In Mineralnie Vodyi he had to jump out of his small car and transfer to one of the last German tanks. We met him one more time during our travels, after which he completely disappeared for the duration of the war.

We moved further and further through the vast expanses of Russia with no definite goal, with few belongings and without money. Our one major desire was to move as far away as possible from the Soviet forces. These eleven months of wanderings I have described in greater detail in my book *After Leningrad,* published in the form of a diary.

In July we were in the Krivoi Rog in the Ukraine. There we fell into the hands of representatives of the German civil authorities who were rounding up able-bodied citizens for work in Germany. That is how we finally arrived at a large military factory, not far from Coblenz on the Rhine. We were placed in a camp in Bendorf for workers from the East. This camp was surrounded by barbed wire and guarded by sentries. It was mostly filled with Ukranian youths between the ages of fifteen and eighteen who had been forceably taken by the Germans and were now working at the factory. The German commander of this camp was loud and constantly shouting at all of us. We lived in that camp for more than a year. On 26 March 1945 the Americans crossed the Rhine at Remagen and seized all of the towns located along its shores, including Bendorf.

Following that day, which is described by me in more detail in my book *Allies On The Rhine,* there were again many anxious days and situations. For example, there was pillaging by the newly freed East workers. These bands stole everything and from everybody they could, and even we became victims of such raids. Exhausted and worn out by our difficulties, we had decided to return to our homeland and went to the transfer camp. We owe our salvation to a young American lieutenant who warned us of what was awaiting the Russian returnees.

The Americans were replaced by the Belgians and the Belgians by the French. This last circumstance, namely the French occupation of this part of Germany, played an enormous role in our lives because it saved us from compulsory repatriation and gave us the opportunity to spend five happy, peaceful years in that charming little city on the Rhine. It replaced my abandoned homeland.

The French had not participated in the Yalta Conference in early 1945 at which Churchill, Roosevelt, and Stalin, upon the demand of the latter, had decided to return to the Soviet Union all those persons forceably taken to Germany for work. Of course Stalin promised to pardon all of his citizens and return all privileges and the right to return to their native villages. This, however, did not occur. Some two million Russians were transferred by the English and American forces to the Soviets and were either shot or sent to "correction" camps in Siberia. No one returned home. Only now, when all the documents kept secret all these years have been opened, has criminal treachery become fully known. In addition to having read about this in books, I have heard much from eyewitnesses.

Once in a plane I entered into conversation with a middle-aged American who was sitting next to me. He told me how, as a young soldier in Germany after the war, he had been sent with other soldiers to accompany Russians who were supposedly joyfully returning to their homeland. When the trucks arrived at a certain bridge in Austria, which led to Soviet-occupied territory, great agitation broke out among the Russian returnees. On the other side of the bridge, Soviet troops, mostly KGB (Soviety security agents) awaited to welcome home their compatriots. Many of the returnees hurled themselves into the water and drowned. Women with children in their arms followed their husbands. The young Americans were terribly disconcerted by this unexpected event. Nonetheless, they continued to carry out their orders. The trucks were emptied and those in them had to cross the bridge on foot toward their own people. Almost immediately thereafter the American soldiers heard shooting. Only then did the criminal act in which they had played an involuntary role become completely clear to them.

The KGB had awaited their citizens to whom had been given the name "collaborators," although the majority of them had still been children and forceably taken from Soviet Russia. From the Soviet viewpoint, they had seen too much and had discovered that over the course of the years in the USSR, they had been fed a lot of lies about the capitalist setup of the Western countries. When they themselves had come in contact with the life of people in those countries, they became dangerous witnesses for the Soviet Union and consequently had to be destroyed.

To our great fortune, and thanks to the aid of the young American mentioned earlier, we were not repatriated. We did not remain in the camp that had been burned to the ground but lived, however, in a private home with a German family.

The arrival in Germany of an American of Russian origin interested in all types of manuscripts and diaries of people who had lived through the war and especially the Leningrad Blockade, decided our future. He took my diary and, upon his return to America, began to arrange a sponsor for me; for without a sponsor it was impossible to get into the United States.

It was difficult for us to leave our nest and all those people who had treated us so well. But at that time, Germany was going through tremendous postwar difficulties, and the problem of food and residence was extremely difficult. There were enormous numbers of refugees from East Germany, and the situation for foreigners was especially difficult in the sense of finding employment. It was impossible to compete with Germans, if only because of the language. Again, we had to make a decision to undertake something new. For me, as always, the stimulus was my children; I was responsible for their future. After much soul-searching and bogged with doubt, I decided with a heavy heart to leave Germany. My uneasiness was no less diminished by the knowledge that my son Dima's departure would be delayed, due to his recent marriage and the birth of a new baby.

On 13 May 1950, as part of a large group of emigrants, Yuri and I boarded the *General Stuart Heintzelman,* the huge military steamer that would take us to America.

# 6

## FIRST STEPS IN A NEW WORLD

*ARRIVAL IN AMERICA, MAY 1950*

Among the passengers there is noise, talk. Everybody is bustling about, animated. We are approaching New York, sailing past the Statue of Liberty. I go up on deck. The same mood takes hold of me, the same mood I had when we sailed from Europe—the fear of the unknown; excitement, agitation, doubt, but also a feeling of joy that a new chapter of life is beginning, and with it the hope for something better.

The last ten years have been years of anxiety, difficult camp years, endless fear. Everybody is expecting something special from America. Not for nothing has America always been imagined to be a wonderful country, unlike anything else.

It is evening. The sun is still high and illuminates the shore beautifully. Autos are stretched out in an unbroken line. But there will be no disembarcation today. It is a holiday—Memorial Day, the 30th of May. One more day to spend on our ark.

The first exhausting day in the new world ended. It was a day full of anxieties and new impressions. The following morning was taken up with the endless procedures of disembarcation requiring the examination of papers and checking of luggage. For Yuri and me it was torture.

How were we to explain anything to the customs officials, when we spoke not a word of English? What little I had known at one time, I had long since forgotten. When it was our turn to have our luggage checked, the only suspicious item we had turned out to be our Leica, the fine German camera in which we had invested all our money—700 marks, roughly $175.

The customs official examined the camera for a long time, moving it from one hand to the other, and all the while asking us questions that we, of course, could not answer. The importation of new cameras was not permitted.

Before our departure I had loaded the camera with film and had been diligently taking pictures throughout the entire voyage, especially when a storm came up and flooded the deck with huge waves. I tried to prove to the strict customs agent that the camera was not new. Speaking no English, I had to explain with my hands, opening the camera and pointing to the film. This, apparently, spoiled many photos. Yuri and I had been terribly afraid they would confiscate the camera, our single treasure. The official must have felt sorry for us, for he did not take it.

Having finished with the official formalities, we began to roam about the huge port building and to converse with others who had arrived on the same ship. Many of the new arrivals were awaiting relatives or friends who had sent them visas and affidavits. I knew that our sponsor was fictitious; he had signed the necessary papers only in order to help us leave Europe. He had no intention of employing us. Thus, Yuri and I were awaiting no one. We had no clear idea where to go from there. The huge port building was humming with activity, and we did not have the painful sensation of loneliness. Some young American women were even treating everyone to doughnuts and coffee.

A representative of the Tolstoy Fund called out for all those who had been registered for the Tolstoy farm and to whom that organization had sent the required papers. Our new friends, the Yavorskis and the Olshevskis, went there; the Samiloviches, mother and son, were met by an entire family of relatives. These were all German Jews who had managed to leave Germany before Hitler's seizure of power. Mrs. Samilovich was married to a German, a member of the Nazi party. After the death of her husband, she decided to move with her son to her relatives in Rhode Island.

They quickly took leave but gave us their address so that we could locate them and then look for work from there, should we decide to do so. This was reassuring. It was during the voyage that Yuri, not affected by the rocking or suffering from seasickness the way I had, became acquainted with these passengers.

The crowd thinned out. More time passed and I began to notice, with a bit of nervousness, that from our huge transport here remained only a small group of people. Now the question of where we should go loomed as a rather serious matter. I still held some hope that Nikholaevskii, who had signed for us, would at the last minute find a more reliable sponsor, a sponsor who would hire us. Since the list of new arrivals had been printed in *Nvoye Russkoye Slovo*, Nikholaevski would have known when we were to arrive in New York.

Nonetheless, I decided to talk with the representative of the Tolstoy Fund, who had finished checking the new arrivals for whom he was responsible and was preparing to take them to the farm where, I hoped, he could also take us. Suddenly, I heard my name on the loudspeaker. I went to the information booth and asked who was calling me. At that moment I noticed a man and woman who were asking the Tolstoy employee something, and the latter pointed to Yuri and me.

Fortunately, Tolstoy and his wife were indeed looking for us. In Germany, several years earlier, we had been receiving packages of clothing. The main organizer of this aid was Tolstoy's wife. Now, from the newspapers, they had learned about our arrival and decided to help us through the initial stages of our relocation.

The Tolstoys told us what, in their opinion, was good news. A mutual acquaintance from Germany had rented an apartment from students who had left for the summer. This apartment was intended for his friends, the Krylov family, who were being detained in Germany because of emigration formalities. This young fellow, Slutsky, had proposed that the Tolstoys put us temporarily in this apartment. Apparently he was sure that I could find work soon and Yuri and I would be leaving the apartment before the arrival of his friends.

Hearing the details I not only was not overjoyed, but terrified. The idea of moving with Yuri into a strange apartment in New York and, what was still worse in a not so good neighborhood—something the Tolstoys did not try to hide from me—not knowing a word of English, did not seem to be the least inviting. This apartment was on the corner of Broadway and 134th Street.

It would have been much better to have gone to the Tolstoy farm with a large group of Russians and work there, until people came to hire persons for professional or clerical work. It was said that Americans often came to the Tolstoy farm and hired those among the refugees who made a favorable impression on them.

The Tolstoys did not agree. This type of selection seemed to them to be humiliating, and they thought I would find work much more quickly living in New York and establishing contacts with various agencies. I had to trust their judgment and experience. With a heavy heart, I gathered our belongings and went with them to the new apartment.

The Tolstoys had been living in America for a long time already; they had their own car and knew the city very well. At first they took us to a huge grocery store and helped us buy the most essential groceries. Then we went further along 134th Street to where our apartment was located.

The first impression will remain for the rest of my life. That section of the city was indeed extremely unattractive. The population was, for the most part, Puerto Rican. There was dirt everywhere: garbage, parts of newspapers, cigarette butts, discarded bits of food. There was a crowd right in the middle of the street: the children were playing ball while cars honked, adding to the already unbelievable noise. From all sides one heard an unfamiliar language, a mixture of Spanish and English.

We entered a yard, dirty just like the street. From the benches covered with garbage came the stench of decay, accentuated by the damp heat. The windows of our small apartment looked out onto the yard. Right in front of the windows was the fire escape stairs, and this terrified me. I kept imagining how easy it would be to come into the apartment through those stairs. What was to stop someone from knocking out the thin glass? En route we had heard quite a few frightening tales about large American cities, especially Chicago and New York. Now I imagined bandits everywhere.

The young fellow who had found this apartment for the Krylovs was waiting for us inside. Apparently my disgust and horror were clearly reflected in my facial expression. Slutsky, having expected delight and gratefulness, noticed the impression it had made. He tried to convince me that it was indeed fine and wonderful to have your own nook, at least at first. He didn't forget also to mention all the American conveniences: the Frigidaire, bathroom, shower. If only he had known with what joy I would have moved into a kitchen, deprived of all these conveniences, only to be with a family where I could converse in a language I knew.

I did not respond to what he was saying, only listened to the unceasing roar of the frightening, huge city. The Tolstoys left after this, promising to visit the next day.

Slutsky remained a while in order to try to raise our spirits. Yuri, looking at me, was also depressed. I asked Slutsky to find us even the smallest room, so that we would not have to remain in this apartment. He promised that he would try, but his tone was none too convincing. In no way did he share my fears and, apparently, thought this was all capriciousness on my part. He soon left.

I kept thinking about distant Germany, the Marx's house, which was dear to my heart. There I was surrounded by friends and acquaintances. Why, why had we come to this unfamiliar country? What would we do here? What was awaiting us?

I took myself in hand because of Yuri—I did not wish to reveal my despair—and began to unpack our belongings and prepare our simple food. Yuri sat quietly, apparently also thinking about why he left Europe, school, his friends, the Bendorf club, and the Marx family, who treated him as one of their own.

And the street did not quiet down. Just the opposite. On that wonderful May evening, no one wanted to sleep in a stuffy apartment. It was at least two o'clock in the morning before we could fall asleep. Everything bothered us, from the noise of the street to the damp heat with which we had come in contact for the first time in our lives. One of my acquaintances from America had warned me, but I had not believed him, thinking he was simply trying to frighten us. In any case, he was at least exaggerating.

It seems to me that never, even during the most severe bombings and shellings, had I been as unhappy as during this first night in America.

After a few hours of uneasy sleep, we were awakened by a loud knock on the door. I decided not to open it, since in any case I could not have made myself understood. The knock was repeated stubbornly. We kept as quiet as mice. After knocking several times, the uninvited visitor finally left.

Not an hour had passed when the stubborn knocking was repeated. Since Slutsky had promised to come not earlier than twelve, I decided not to pay any attention. The visitor continued to knock for quite some time. Despite all his attempts, there was no reaction on our part.

Right at twelve I opened the door to the cautious knock of Slutsky. Yuri and I rushed to tell him about all the horrors we had experienced. He agreed that the region was indeed not desirable.

I again implored him to find us another shelter promising that I would accept any work, as a servant, cook, governess, anything to get out of this building, out of this dreadful apartment with all of its American conveniences of which we had been deprived in Germany, and where we had been a thousand times happier. Even our "East" worker barracks seemed to us now to be a paradise. There we had not been alone. We had been surrounded with our Russian girls and boys. We remembered those trusty fellows, Vasya and Petya, who had come for us during each bombing, if they were not at work, trying to rescue our belongings and cheering us up just with their presence. Here, with the exception of those hours when Slutsky appeared, we were completely alone. This was worse than being on an uninhabited island, since from the street there was this constant unfamiliar language, shouting, and the honking of cars. The huge unfamiliar city roared unceasingly, filling us with fear. There was no way out for the time being. We had to bear it and wait until our situation changed.

Our only support, Slutsky, suggested we go out onto the street and visit a few of his acquaintances who, perhaps, might be able to advise us as to what we should do. With this hope we went out and were immediately in this Babylon called New York. Fortunately, however, on the streets we did not feel the horror that had oppressed us in the apartment.

The weather was wonderful; there were people everywhere. On Broadway, along which we first walked, there were only foreign languages to be heard, especially Russian. This immediately raised our spirits.

As far as the friendly counsel from Slutsky's friends was concerned, it was a complete disaster. Some were not at home; others, already spoiled by American conveniences, had quickly forgotten camp conditions and were not inclined to share their quarters with us.

One Russian priest offered us $25, but I refused. I did not wish to begin life in America on charity. In an empty toothpaste tube I had a reserve of $100, purchased gradually in Germany in preparation for our possible departure. With such capital I considered ourselves rich. The primary need at this moment was not money, however, but shelter for several days until I could find work.

We had to return home with dampened spirits. Slutsky, despite all our ruses to detain him a bit longer, left, promising to return the following morning. Again we spent the night in anxiety. And in the morning there was again the knocking on the door, and our answer was the silence of the grave.

Five tortuous days passed. As though by established order the same routine continued each day. In the morning somebody would hang endlessly on our door. Later, Slutsky would appear and take us by subway through all New York, giving us advice on how to find work. He would bring newspapers, and we could not read them. He himself would investigate ads of employment agencies.

My moral was low. Finally, on the sixth day, I implored Slutsky to come as early as possible and find out who was banging on our door every day. The answer to this problem was most unexpected and comical. The banging was by newspaper boys, milkmen, and others, to whom those students who had sublet the apartment for the summer still owed money.

Slutsky, who also spoke English quite poorly since he had arrived only a few months before, managed to explain to our uninvited guests that we had no relationship with the debtors and we had not opened the door simply because we didn't know a single word of English.

Thank goodness that that was taken care of! Now Yuri and I gathered our courage and on the seventh day, not even awaiting Slutsky's arrival, went to Times Square where there were a number of employment agencies. This we did on foot, from 134th to 42nd Street. One can just imagine how we looked when we got there. But all was in vain. There were many requests for domestics, but requirements were a knowledge of English and someone without children. Disappointed, we went back (but this time by subway) to our fantastic apartment.

Two more days of fruitless searching and then suddenly we came upon an ad in the Russian newspaper by a Russian agency. They were looking for a maid in a hotel-restaurant, some thirty-five miles from New York. We went to the agency. A nice Russian gentleman, an employee of the agency, cautioned us that it would be difficult and that we would not last long. They were tired of sending people there. However, there was no other way out and we decided to meet the owner.

At nine o'clock on the morning of the 9th of June, Yuri and I were in the huge vestibule of an elegant hotel. We waited. A tall pretty woman appeared. She gave the appearance of being very decisive; behind her was a small old woman. The lady showered me immediately with questions such as "Have you ever worked as a maid? Are you familiar with household appliances? Do you know how to make beds?" The last question really upset me. Was it possible that in America there was some new discovery about which I had never heard? To the question, had I ever been a servant I decided to answer indirectly. Although I had never been one, having had a family in Russia I had some knowledge about cleaning an apartment and washing dishes. About my college studies and peda-gogical activities, and especially about my knowledge of French, I kept silent, fortunately.

Everything was going rather smoothly until the owner's glance fell on Yuri. "And who is he?" was the extremely unfriendly question. "This is my son," I answered timidly. The lady's facial expression immediately changed and she said irritatedly, "No. There can be no question of taking her with a son," and turned and headed toward another room. The old lady quickly walked up to me and whispered, "Wait a bit. Don't go away."

Yuri and I sat down and exchanged glances. It would be interesting to know what would happen next. Not even five minutes had passed when both women returned and the young one glanced at me and said, "Where are your things? Let's move. There's no time to lose. Today's Friday." What the significance was of Friday, I found out only later. For it was on Friday that all the guests arrived to spend the weekend in the country. The old woman smiled with understanding and seizing the moment whispered that the other candidate for this "select" position had failed the interview. Thus our chances had risen.

We got our suitcases en route, left a note on the door for Slutsky, and happily left both the apartment and that section where we had spent nine such unpleasant days.

### CROTON HEIGHTS

Our future employer was not very talkative and was busy driving the car which, to be fair, she did very well. Her mother, a sweet old lady who took our unenviable situation to heart, was somewhat intimidated by her daughter and also did not talk much. The car radio was playing wild music, and we were being driven with unaccustomed speed. Along both sides of the road were magnificent views with many rocks, thick woods, green meadows, and pretty houses. We looked at everything with great interest.

Finally we entered a forest or huge park and went up a mountain. The auto stopped in front of a two-story gray wooden building, around which was a large expanse of neatly cut meadow. Further down there were tall trees in a park. This was the country hotel and restaurant where we would have to work.

Across from the main building was a rather large garage and above it an apartment. Mrs. Kochubey, the owner, explained that the employees lived in this apartment and that there was also a room available for us. Our nearest neighbor would be an old cook with whom we would share a bedroom. In the lower floor, next to the garage, lived the gardener and his wife. All the employees were Russian. This was a great relief. At least there would be no difficulty with the language.

We dragged our suitcases up the narrow stairway. Despite the simplicity of our new apartment—a small room with one window—it seemed a gift from heaven to me. While we were unpacking and arranging things, a small gray-haired old man appeared in the doorway. This was our neighbor, the cook. He came to get acquainted with his new neighbors and colleagues. From him we found out all the details of Croton life and, although he did not paint it in rosy colors, difficulty did not frighten me and my spirits did not sink.

That very day, after getting acquainted with the owner, a nice, good-natured gentleman about fifty-five, I began to carry out my duties. I was told that on such days as the end of the week, beginning with Friday when the guests gather, I would have to help the waiter in the evening, for by himself he could not handle everything. That evening I also had to wash the dishes and prepare the salads. I already knew that our employer did not like questions; one had to know how to handle everything. Thus, I did not ask but did everything as I felt it should be done. It was fortunate that in the bustle no one paid any attention to me.

The waiter was rushing in and out of the dining hall with huge trays and a shining face. Obviously he was already anticipating some good tips from such a flood of guests. There was little pleasure for me from this. All I got was a mountain of dirty dishes containing uneaten food. After all the years of wartime hunger and the post-war years in

Germany, it was strange and difficult to look at this great amount of food which was to be simply thrown into the garbage.

There was no time to think about it all. The waiter kept bringing more and more dishes; and it was impossible to keep up with his pace. I got weak from the unbearable heat. The sweat was pouring from my face. Not only was there no fan or air-conditioning, but just a few feet away was the scorching hot oven. Across from my place of work, the sink and the dishwasher, was a window to the garden. The damp heat wafted from there too. In the darkness of a tree I could see Yuri, whom the strict manageress had forbidden in the kitchen. He was sadly observing his mother in her new role of dishwasher in a "princely" hotel.

Involuntarily I recalled the words I had said to the cheerful Americans on the commission in Rastatt in Germany. I had indeed guessed what my unchanging future would be in the "promised" land, to which we were trying to go.

The next morning began the learning of how to make beds, to which Mrs. Kochubey had given such great importance. I was an extremely mediocre student. The princess, reddening and dissatisfied with my lack of comprehension, forced me a fifth time to remake her old mother's bed. All the other beds were occupied by guests, for whom such a lesson would have seemed quite strange. I finally mastered this art.

In so far as the household appliances went, such as the vacuum cleaner, Mrs. Kochubey had no doubt as to my ability to use them. I decided not to inform her that neither in the Soviet Union nor in postwar Germany had I had the occasion to become familiar with them. Fortunately for me, Yuri was permitted to help me carry the heavy vacuum cleaner, and in the technical operation he was much better informed than I. The vacuum cleaner began to work, deafening all the guests of the second-floor, who had not yet managed to leave their rooms. The work was getting done. The bathrooms were cleaned, the beds made. Mrs. Kochubey had no time to check on how my work was progressing. She was busy bustling about the kitchen and the guests.

Before we finished the cleaning, it was already time to serve lunch. Yuri went to help the gardener gather flowers and put out the chaise lounges for the guests who liked to rest in the open after a full lunch.

My place by the dishwasher was occupied by the gardener's wife. The waitress work was easier, if only it had not been for the English language. There were many misunderstandings this first day of my work. The guest would ask for pepper, and I would bring a glass; instead of a napkin, salt. I was often rescued by the waiter, a young man of Polish-Jewish origin who had also abandoned his motherland and decided to settle in America. The guests for the most part were generous toward my errors. They would ask me how long I had been in America and were delighted by my beautiful explanations in the form of my ten fingers.

Many of them spoke Russian, some French and German. They would shower me with questions about life in Germany, about the war, about all our adventures. It was necessary to remain at tables to the great annoyance of Mrs. Kochubey who had been observing my activities from the adjoining parlor. In her opinion, a servant should not do this—but I naively thought that it was not polite to go away from such nice people without satisfying their curiosity.

The result of the first day of work was unbelievable. The pocket of my white apron was stuffed with one and even five dollar bills. All of this I had to give to my headwaiter. He, however, after counting all his wealth, paid me a certain percent. This was the established rule. I was very well satisfied, since even the 10 percent I received seemed to me unbelievable wealth.

During the afternoon I was able to rest for one hour. Instead of lying down to sleep, I took my typewriter and quickly dashed down my first impressions of my life in America. In New York City, in that horrible apartment, I was simply unable to concentrate; here, despite my fatigue, my mood was much more cheerful. Yuri did not lie down; he was extremely interested in everything about our new life.

The guests, when they were out strolling, were drawn into conversation with him. Yuri quite willingly satisfied their curiosity. Most of the guests were Russian Jews who had been living in New York for a long time. They liked this restaurant very much because the cook prepared all types of Russian dishes fantastically well, dishes they had become unaccustomed to, living here in America.

A few days after our arrival in Croton Heights, Mrs. Kochubey summoned me and inquired what I intended to do with Yuri. She thought that he should be placed in a summer camp where he could learn English more quickly, being among other children. I was quite satisfied with this but had not the faintest idea of where to find such a place.

On my day off I went to New York to Nikholaevski, the man who had signed the papers enabling us to come to America, to ask his advice. Not finding him there, I told his secretary, Burgina, all our troubles about enrolling Yuri in a camp.

The conditions in which Yuri found himself were not at all suitable for a boy his years, especially since surrounded by Russians, he would never learn English. Burgina immediately found a solution. She knew of a camp not far from New York that opened the 1st of July, and it was possible to enroll Yuri. The cost for the summer was $100 which she offered to pay; and I accepted on the condition that when I had earned that money in the fall, I would give it back to her. This was a wonderful way out of our dilemma.

In addition to the money for the stay at camp, various articles of clothing were also needed. Thus my cash reserve, brought in the bottom of an empty tube of toothpaste, melted away that very day. Burgina advised me to talk with Kerensky who had arranged loans for refugees in a certain bank. I decided to try my luck and went to see him after telephoning to be sure he was there. He was extremely kind, immediately giving me a $100 bill against my signature and asking me about the details of our arrival and work. As far as the loan was concerned, he said I could pay it back according to my ability. He did not express any satisfaction about my work in the princely hotel and advised me to study English intensively, so that I could change employment.

In general he was very nice and, fortunately for me, was not interested in my maiden name. Being in the forth State Parliament (Duma), where my father also was, Kerensky had been my father's fierce foe. After this consultation with Kerensky, I still had to make a few personal purchases for myself. Because of the heat and dampness, nothing I had brought with me from Germany was suitable to wear here.

All the way back I kept thinking about the invaluable service Burgina had done for me, having lent a considerable sum of money to a completely unknown person, and that even without a signature. Again I was lucky. In America, too, it was possible to meet people who were willing to help. While I was at Kerensky's, Burgina phoned to find out where and when she should bring Yuri.

Happy with the day's success and loaded down with packages of clothing, I returned to Croton and informed our new managers that Yuri would have to stay two more weeks there. We agreed that they would deduct the cost of his food from my weekly pay of $20. The question had been resolved to our mutual satisfaction.

Yuri tried in every way to be useful both in the hotel and in the garden. He helped the old gardener for whom it was difficult to carry anything heavy; he would run to fulfill any request and very soon he had won the heart of Mrs. Kochubey. As a result, I was informed that there would be no deductions for Yuri's food.

The main thing that made life in Croton pleasant was the regular return on weekends of certain guests from New York. We became special friends with the couples Kassirer and Stein. They were the most frequent guests, never missing a weekend. Kassirer's wife was a native of

St. Petersburg; he was from Berlin. They had come to America not long before Hitler seized power and now were well established in New York. He was the vice president of a large company; she was the manager of a division of the public library. On Friday, we would impatiently await their arrival and, although we had little time to converse with them, we would use every free minute to spend with these fine people.

Also good friends were the Stein couple. I remember how he would recite Onegin for us, to the great amazement and delight of Yuri. And there were other guests who left a very favorable impression. Many of them had experienced similar unpleasantness in Russia. For me, people have always been the most important part of my life. I have become convinced of this these last years. In moments of complete despair and in seemingly hopeless situations, a kind word and the support of friends has changed everything. And life would become easier and happier.

It was the same here. Thanks to the people around us, even this unaccustomed and difficult work no longer seemed so forbidding as during the first days. I began to face the future with much greater cheer.

At the beginning of July, I took Yuri to camp. It was a sad day for me; we had never been separated before. Alas! It was necessary and there was nothing to do but accept the situation. Our bosses, the old cook, and some of the guests, generously rewarded him. He left a real capitalist, according to our thinking. He was carrying a suitcase of essential clothing. The camp required all kinds of things in such a quantity as Yuri had never in his life had. I myself was amazed but, according to the list given me by Burgina, I was to buy a pile of socks, shorts, blue trousers, a quantity of shirts and so forth. It was unthinkable that Yuri feel deprived in comparison with the other children.

With Yuri gone, life became dull. I gradually grew accustomed to the work and to the appliances which had been new to me.

One extremely unpleasant event happened to me during this time. I had never previously used the washing machines. The first days I was afraid to put too many towels in it, the towels being done at the hotel. The larger linens were taken to the laundry. I did this all satisfactorily. One day in the middle of July, after a large gathering of guests, I loaded the machine until it was entirely full and sat down nearby to recite English words, something I tried to do every spare minute. Suddenly, I heard a strong cracking noise and the machine stopped. Mrs. Kochubey came rushing upon my call and was absolutely beside herself. A mechanic had to be called and, since he didn't appear at once, we had to take the entire pile of dirty towels to the neighboring town. I was very upset, since obviously the accident was entirely my fault. I had not made such a good servant.

With Yuri gone, I began to go to New York on my day off. I saw many acquaintances with whom we traveled here from Europe. All of them had managed to find work. It was interesting to share impressions about living conditions in this new country. More often I went to the Jaworskys and the Olshevskys, with whom we were so close during our stay in Rastatt.

I also dropped in frequently at the Tolstoy Fund and spoke with Aleksandra Lvovna, the daughter of our famous Lev Tolstoy. When she found out where and how I was working, Aleksandra became indignant. Why did I not try to find employment as a teacher of Russian? Or, at least, somewhere in an office? "You dreamed up the idea of being a servant," she said in irritation, adding "Indeed, you'll probably try to be a good housemaid."

I objected saying that I could go nowhere, not knowing English and not being able to understand what was said to me. In order to entertain and distract her, I began to relate some of the unbelievable anecdotes which had livened my life at Croton. Aleksandra Lvovna calmed down and laughed heartily. But afterwards she again began to try to convince me that I had to learn English as quickly as possible. "Only then will your years in Leningrad University not be lost." I, of course, agreed with her; but for the time being I could see no rainbows.

About this time Laura's parents, the Krylovs, and her sister managed to arrive in the U.S. All of them settled into that infamous apartment Slutsky had rented for us. It was not so bad for the Krylovs because there were three of them, including a man. In addition, Laura's sister, Rima, already spoke some English. All of this gave them a great advantage over us. I visited them and was already finding that the apartment was not as repulsive as it had appeared to me during the first days of our stay.

Dima and his wife arrived at the beginning of August with their baby, and I was given a day off from Croton Heights in order to go meet them. And thus the family had come together in the new continent. Europe became a memory.

I had to meet Yuri on September 1. During the entire summer of his stay in camp, I was able to visit him only twice. This was so because the camp was rather far from New York and from Croton and it was quite a trip, taking almost the entire day. It was almost impossible to be absent from work for any amount of time because of their personnel shortage.

On that 1st of September, Dima and I went down to the pier since the children were brought down the Hudson by boat. We waited and waited. Many children, met by their parents, had already left the ship but Yuri was nowhere to be seen. I began to get nervous when suddenly a boy ran up to me trying to explain something. I immediately decided that something had happened to Yuri and tried to understand what was going on.

It is impossible to describe my feelings of both surprise and horror when I realized that the boy who had run up to me was Yuri himself. It turned out that just a few days before his departure he had gotten infected with poison ivy, something entirely unknown to me. It had spread over his face, and he looked like he was wearing a mask. Huge ears protruded from this mask, as did a puffed-up neck, and everything was covered with red blotches. I had been so happy, awaiting a healthy and cheerful boy; and suddenly I had this disappointment. Yuri tried to calm me, saying that it was not dangerous and that it would soon pass. I was, however, inconsolable.

Upon our return to Croton, Yuri had to spend several days in his room since he could not show himself to the guests in that condition. I was only hoping that it would disappear by the beginning of the term in the school where he had been registered.

In six days he had recovered from that disgusting affliction—but I had become infected. My hands were covered with blotches, but my face was unaffected. I had to serve in the restaurant with bandaged hands which, while not very pleasant, was not as disgusting as if my hands had remained exposed. This infection did not leave me very quickly, and from my hands it spread over my whole body. I couldn't sleep at nights and in the daytime I would be sleepy and tired. Some people, I am told, are not at all affected by poison ivy. I, however, am apparently extremely sensitive to it.

The entire month of September, such a beautiful fall month, was completely spoiled for me, first by Yuri's infection, then by mine. My thoughts kept returning to Europe. We had never had comparable weather there; we never had to suffer such a humid heat, especially like that upon our arrival in New York. In Europe there had been no poison grass which caused such discomfort. In Russia and in Germany we had roamed through the woods from morning to night, gathering mushrooms and berries, and never were afraid to touch anything. Here, one couldn't even go out into the park. You always had to look to see whether this grass was around.

Yuri quickly adapted to school and was already speaking English rather well. As soon as I got over the poison ivy infection we went to see Nikholaevski, and I gratefully returned to Burgina the $100 which she had lent to me in June. They were amazed by Yuri's success with English.

He was also well liked in school, both by the teachers and by the pupils. They tried to help him with the language. He was my translator since, unfortunately, my knowledge was scarcely increasing. Too many of the guests were Europeans and I did not have to speak English with them.

We were preparing for the long, last weekend of the season, Thanksgiving day. All the rooms had been reserved in advance. Mrs. Kochubey bought all types of food; the owner took care of the drinks, while the cook prepared fantastic pies and all types of dishes. We were awaiting all our new friends.

Everything began on Wednesday. One guest after another arrived. The Kassirers brought us a huge quantity of gifts which raised our mood still further. Everything went fine until Thursday evening. Then, completely unexpectedly, about six in the evening, a strong wind came up followed by a heavy rain. Soon the wind turned into a real hurricane. All the windows in the house were shaking and the trees were cracking and breaking. I could never have imagined such a tempest.

Everyone's mood changed. It was dangerous to drive home. Therefore, everyone decided to remain and wait out the storm. It seemed almost impossible to remain in the upper story because of the howling and raging of the wind. Everybody crowded into the parlor and around the bar in the basement. There the fireplace burned pleasantly.

Toward night the storm had not only not diminished but had increased to such an extent that it had ripped off all wires and the electricity in the building went out, almost creating a panic. The old trees in the park were falling with a crash. (The following day we counted thirty of them!)

We spent the night anxiously, but toward morning the storm quieted down. The sun appeared, illuminating a sad picture. It was impossible to drive down a single road leading from the hotel because of the heaps of branches and the huge trees that had fallen. Everything appeared as though there had been a battle.

Taking advantage of a free moment, Yuri, the cook, and I went out to look over the area around our hotel. The cook was more than seventy years old, but he assured me that although he had lived in many countries, he had never in his whole life seen anything like it. What unbelievable natural phenomena there are in America!

This storm influenced the owners to change a decision they had made. Until the storm they had wanted Yuri, the cook, and me, to remain in Croton during the winter months which they usually spent in Florida. This idea had appealed to us very much. We were good friends with the cook, and Yuri's school was not very far away. New York could be visited easily, and in the winter there was skiing and skating. We were even thinking about setting up a large Christmas tree in the parlor and inviting our friends. Now all our plans went down the drain.

The storm had caused such tremendous damage that there was repair work to be done everywhere. The Kochubeys were trying to find workers to repair the damages. They were also concerned about the possibility of a repetition of such a storm and about our helplessness in such a situation. They therefore decided to close up the hotel and advised us to place an ad in the local newspaper that a woman with a son was seeking three months employment. Nobody answered this ad.

Since Yuri had aready become accustomed to this school, I thought it might not be a bad idea to leave him in Yorktown, a small village where this school was located, and put him in a boarding house run by acquaintances of the Kochubeys. I would, in the meantime, try to find employment in New York. Yuri was absolutely against such an arrangement. He did not want to live in a strange house and be separated from me. I also did not like this prospect, but for the time being there was no other way out.

I went to New York and looked for a room. I found a small, dark room with a Russian family on 80th Street West.

The Kochubeys made me the following proposition: if I would return to them in March, that is after the three months they would be in Florida, they would pay me $100 a month. I, of course, agreed. This was already a great support. For Yuri I had to pay $50 a month, and my room cost $30. I would look for some kind of temporary work in addition. Once I had found work, Yuri would come every Friday to spend the weekend with me.

In search of employment, I happened to come across one of the Croton guests who suggested that I come live at her estate which was not far from New York. She said that Yuri could come every Friday, and he would no longer have to ride alone to New York. I would have to help around the house and, in addition, would receive $75 a month. This seemed like quite an acceptable proposition and I agreed.

On the first day of my stay at Mrs. Wolf's I realized I had made a stupid mistake. This woman, a German, was being supported by an American and behaved as a rich and willful tyrant. She was the complete boss on this estate; her friend had an apartment in New York. She was surrounded by servants and "parasites." Having come from a poor family, she was intoxicated with her wealth and the power she had over people dependent on her. The cook was an Italian woman who spoke almost no English, although she was rather independent thanks to her ability to cook so well. Mrs. Wolf's greatest pleasure was to eat well.

She never gave a thought to dieting, although I had never seen such a fat woman in all my life. The cunning cook had quickly won her over.

In addition to the cook there were two male employees. One of them served as bartender and entertained the lady with endless stories. That was his entire responsibility. She ordered him around but was nice to him. The second gentleman was about forty-five and considered superfluous to the household. And indeed, I too found him absolutely unnecessary. To both of us she showed her real character. My duties were very unclear, which was especially unpleasant to me.

The lazy Mrs. Wolf slept late in the mornings. During her sleep, no noise was permitted and I could not use the vacuum cleaner in the reception rooms. It was awkward not to do anything, so I tried to give the impression that I was busy. The Italian woman watched me disapprovingly. At twelve o'clock I had to be on the alert in order that, heaven forbid!, I wouldn't miss the moment when the bell from the bedroom rang. The bell meant that the mistress had awakened and was demanding breakfast.

My duty was to bring a tray with coffee and the large breakfast which she ate in bed. Sometimes this was at twelve o'clock, sometimes at 3:00 o'clock! The breakfast procedure was endlessly long and, in my opinion, absolutely idiotic. The Italian woman taught me how to prepare the orange juice, how the coffee was to be made (according to all her rules), how to fold the napkin just so, to be sure that under no circumstances were the eggs cooked more than three minutes—and so forth. Heaven forbid that one should forget some detail! For then our mistress could not restrain her temper and would curse, using the most extreme words. Most important, however, the entire next day would be spent in a stormy atmosphere; and it would be better not to have her see you. However, since being seen by her was unavoidable, it meant that the day was ruined for everyone in the house.

When I went with the tray I was boiling inside. My only wish was to empty the tray onto that fat torso of hers, she who imagined herself a queen just because her friend had millions that others did not have. The tray was set on a special table across Mrs. Wolf's bed. Sleepy, unkempt, and unwashed, she would begin to eat. She demanded not only that I be present for her meal, but that I entertain her with conversation. It never occurred to her to ask me to sit down.

After the long procedure of breakfast, I had to clean her room in a special manner and then go downstairs to set the table for dinner. One of her "parasites" taught me how to set the table just so for dinner and how to serve the dishes to her satisfaction. The same feeling I had in the morning—of wanting to dump the tray on her—remained with me. How I would have liked to have emptied the dinner dishes on her!

The dinner process dragged on for about two hours and sometimes even longer. After I had cleared the table and eaten supper with the Italian woman, I was already so tired from the stupid manner in which the day had been spent that I only wanted to go to bed at night.

But there was one more thing to be remembered: the preparation of Mrs. Wolf's bedroom for the night. Only three or four hours earlier I had put everything into order, but now I again had to prepare the bed for the lady's sleep. The Italian woman showed me how to spread out the nightgown prettily, how to turn down the sheet, and how to place Mrs. Wolf's slippers so that she could put her feet into them without bending over. And under no circumstances could I forget to place a pitcher of cold water at her bedside.

All these foolish demands from this coarse and uneducated creature deeply annoyed me. Here was a woman who, because of her lover's money, could attain authority over people and create such humiliating situations, only because they lacked money. (Mrs. Wolf, apparently on the recommendation of her millionaire friend, was a physical education teacher at Columbia University.)

Several times I forgot to carry out the full procedure for the bedroom preparation, and then I roused her anger. The Italian woman would wake me if I had fallen asleep in the evening and would send me to do everything according to the established order. But this Italian made my life miserable no less than did the mistress. For example, in the morning if she found me cleaning rooms with a dictionary in my hands (which was usually the case), she would be beside herself.

How I held out there for three weeks I simply do not know. At the beginning of January, I announced that I wanted to leave, using as a pretext the necessity of studying English. I moved to New York and enrolled in an adult school. Yuri implored me to take him with me. It was more pleasant for me, too, for both of us to be together; I took a room on 108th Street, near the park, again with a Russian family. This time the room was larger and lighter. Yuri was transferred to a school close to the apartment, and our two month stay in New York began.

I decided to study the language seriously. In the morning I went to a private teacher and, in the evening, to adult courses. In the intervals, when Yuri was out of school, we would go to the movies and sit there sometimes through the second show, if I had no evening classes. At that time the films cost thirty cents at almost all the theaters on Broadway. Yuri already knew English very well and understood everything.

On Sunday I would walk through the museums. I especially liked the Frick collection, which Mrs. Kassirer had shown to me. I had gone there with her almost every Sunday when they had concerts, which made it even more pleasant. We received invitations from various persons with whom we had become acquainted in Croton. This time we actually enjoyed our life in New York rather than being frightened as we were upon our arrival from Europe.

One time Mrs. Burgina suggested we take Yuri to a chess club, something he had wanted to do for a long time. The three of us went and were not greeted cordially by the club manager who greeted us with a demand for $10 as entry fees. But Yuri became a member of the club and began to go there often. One evening two weeks later, I went there for him and the manager greeted me with a friendly smile and gave me my $10 back, showering me with compliments about Yuri's playing. He told me that he did not wish to take money from such a talented boy and considered it an honor to have such a lad in his club. Yuri was so happy, and I was in seventh heaven.

I found I had to look for some kind of supplementary work. It was difficult to live on the $100 paid to me by the Kochubeys. Through acquaintances I found a job in a music office, where I was hired only because of my relationship with the composer Skrjabin, for my English was still very weak. The work was the most boring work imaginable. For entire days I would be busy with the card index, now writing something down, now looking for something. I would begin to fall asleep and would jump up and run to the lavatory to splash cold water on my face to wake myself up.

I soon became convinced that such monotonous work was not for me and paradoxically would dream about the arrival of the Kochubey family and working for them as a servant and waitress. At least then I was moving all the time, and with such work there could be no possibility of falling asleep on the job. The only thing now was that I had no desire to leave New York, an interesting and lively city which was a long way from the city it was to become in ten years. At that time, Yuri and I still walked around everywhere, even returning late at night.

Soon we had to change our quarters; our landlords were moving to Colorado. My English teacher advised us to take a room with a Russian widow. This woman was lonely and bored and had been searching for a compatible tenant. To find somebody to live with her was rather difficult, since she had one of the very old New York apartments that looked more like a corridor. The rooms were arranged one after the other: kitchen, dining room, the owner's bedroom (the last two with no windows) and the last room given to us, with windows onto the street. The residents had to go through all the rooms, including Mrs. Ivanova's bedroom. The problem did not bother me much, and Yuri and I moved there. The landlady turned out to be a very sweet person, about fifty years old. She had just lost her husband and, oppressed by loneliness, was looking first for a tenant (fortunately she found me), and then a husband.

The latter search was a bit complicated. Mrs. Ivanova was not distinguished by beauty, and she was not wealthy. Her age also was not especially appealing to prospective suitors. What this lady did not think of! She paid $30 to a special agency that was to help her in the search for a husband. Then she began to go to a restaurant on Broadway famed for such contacts. She would place ads in the Russian newspaper.

Several times the agency arranged dates with suitors who were also enrolled with them; however, during my stay with her she had no success. Sometimes when we came home there would be a suspicious looking person in her apartment. I would rush past into my own room and lock the door. Fortunately for us all, everything passed quite calmly. However, a husband was not found.

On the 5th of March, 1951 we left. Some two weeks later, when we dropped in at her place, I found her beaming. A bald, scrawny fellow of undetermined age was sitting in our former room which had been transformed into a parlour. This fellow was introduced as her husband. Our departure had, obviously, hastened the event.

Later on I learned that things didn't work out well with this spouse. He soon became ill and died. The inconsolable widow again set out in search of a husband and found one, an old man who formerly had been an eye doctor. I met him at a party put on by the New York association of doctors. She introduced us. They both had a lot of free time and, since they both liked to travel, were often on the go. Although I did not express my fears, of course, I thought that she would not be able to enjoy family life very long.

Thanks to my acquaintance with Mrs. Ivanova, I learned about the loneliness of women—something which is widespread in America. Since husbands usually die earlier, New York is flooded with lonely women of all ages.

In Russia and in Europe it is a different matter. Families are closer. The chilren live with their parents even after finishing their studies and often after marriage as well. It is not that easy to find apartments. Often sisters and brothers live together and even the grandfathers and gradmothers who, during my stay in the Soviet Union and even now I hear, are not sent to old folks homes. The older folks have some very limited obligations; they train the grandchildren. In America the picture is different. Here there is no shortage of living quarters. Often the married couple take up a whole house by themselves. One dies and the other remains alone and suffers loneliness. This is especially difficult for Europeans not used to such circumstances.

It was at the beginning of March, when I was living at Mrs. Ivanova's, that I received the news that Varya and her son were moving to America. Even though she had worked in Germany all this time, and even though her son's father was German and planning to remain there, she, nonetheless, had decided to move to America. I went to meet her at the dock after first arranging for her to get some money from the Literary Fund to help her through the first weeks in this country.

*CROTON HEIGHTS, 1951*

Yuri and I returned to Croton as though we were going home, and there we happily greeted all the inhabitants. I had long ago forgiven all the minor unpleasantnesses and the barbs which I had had to endure from Mrs. Kochubey. Her tender concern and love for Yuri had more than compensated for the other. She adored him, and this of course changed my attitude toward her completely.

The owner, as usual, was very kind, the waiter Pavel was merry, the old cook did not conceal his joy to be together with everyone again at work. The mother had been bored in Florida and lovingly was arranging her room in the hotel. Everything went its usual course. The weather, moreover, was wonderful, and it smelled of spring. Everything was being busily prepared for the opening.

I, as though I had never done anything else in my life, was busy with the vacuum cleaner and the dust cloths, so that the hotel would again take on its proper appearance. Yuri was enrolled in school in Yorktown, where he felt a million times better than in New York. There he had had to put up with attacks by hooligans who had wanted to take away his watch. Only the chance appearance of the teacher saved him from one such attack. In the Yorktown school everyone greeted him cordially, from the teachers to the last student. In addition to the warm feelings they had for him, he aroused their interest, for as a foreigner in this school he was unique.

On the 24th of March the opening of the hotel was celebrated. Many guests had gathered and we greeted them like friends and close relatives. The atmosphere was most cordial. The work in no way frightened me. Among the guests were newcomers with whom Yuri soon established cordial relations. I especially remember one charming, elderly Russian

Jew who had lived for a long time in France where he was known as the king with pearls and emeralds. (He had the largest business of the latter.) He and his wife were always very nice to us. They still remain in my memory as a very pleasant reminder of that time.

This season there were far fewer anecdotes caused by my insufficient knowledge of English. Despite everything, I had managed to learn something of English during my stay in New York. The one who had definitely changed toward me for the worse was my employer of three weeks, Mrs. Wolf, who obviously had not forgiven me the poor quality of my work at her estate. She punished me with low tips. I no longer received $15 for serving late suppers, as I formerly had, but had to be satisfied with two. She received special attention in the hotel. Since she refused to eat dinner or supper in the general dining room when there were a lot of people, she would always come when the guests were no longer seated and take up a large table. Often I stood there until the late hours surrounded by her parasites. Frequently I would put several chairs together and would fall asleep in the kitchen. However, I could not leave and go to my room until she was finished.

Some of the guests, especially the Germans, came with a specific purpose—to play chess with Yuri. Yuri had already won some fame as an invincible chess player. Mrs. Kochubey, thanks to her affection for Yuri, did not object to such infringements on the established rules.

We went to New York far less frequently now and spent our free days either in Croton or with the Germans who lived nearby. Sometimes we would go to eat in Yorktown.

According to the strict rules of the Kochubeys, the employees were not allowed to eat in the hotel restaurant on their days off. The cook, with whom we had an especially good relationship, would always bring some special dish to our room, concealing this, of course, from the mistress.

Being especially good-hearted the cook opposed the rules established by Mrs. Kochubey. He was a remarkable person. From his relatively small income, he would send money every month to his friends and acquaintances who had not yet managed to leave Europe. He himself, after his departure from Russia, had been a lawyer for many years in Yugoslavia but had decided to give up his profession and good position in order to become a cook in America. Europe had seemed to him to be rather hopeless because of the nearness of the Soviet Union and the possibility of falling under the Communist dominion from which he had fled.

The summer passed quickly without any special occurrences.

September arrived. On one of my free days when I had gone to New York to visit the Jaworskys, I found that our friend Mr. Jaworsky had moved to Syracuse to teach the Russian language at a newly opened school for airmen at the university.

This led me to think about trying my luck there. First I went to Aleksandra Lvovna Tolstoy for advice. She dampened my spirits by telling me that because of the great number of candidates, the school had ceased hiring. I returned to Croton; but, nonetheless, I decided to go to Syracuse and find out on the spot.

My next day off I took Yuri as a good luck charm and went to Syracuse for an interview with the director of the program. While I was waiting in the reception room, his secretary tried to discourage me by pointing out that she had at least one hundred applications and that there was not a single position open at the time. She advised me not to waste my time and not to wait for Mr. Menu. This did not fit into my plans. After such a long trip, it seemed to me simply idiotic to go away without seeing the director.

Yuri and I, undisturbed by her unfriendly glances, continued to wait. Finally we were called to the director. After questioning me about my education, about my work in the Soviet Union, and about my present situation, the director repeated what the secretary had said about the great number of applicants and the small number of positions available. He was not at all encouraging. Nonetheless, I left him my address and telephone number in Croton, and Yuri and I returned home somewhat downcast.

It was not easy to tell the owners and the employees about our lack of success but, apparently, no one was surprised. They thought that I had been somewhat over-confident and was expecting quite a bit to get a positon at a military school. I had to endure many moments of wounded pride the next day when I was doing the cleaning, washing dishes, laundering, etcetera. The small bit of hope which had flashed by had disappeared.

Well, I thought, it looks as though I shall be stuck in the role of servant just as many other refugees who have come to America. I consoled myself with the thought that I had not expected to be an exception. Why should I now despair?

One morning about a week after our trip to Syracuse, I was cleaning the house when I was called to the telephone. Not accustomed to calls, I was even a bit alarmed. Imagine my amazement when I heard the voice of the director of the Syracuse program, Mr. Menu, inviting me to begin work immediately as an instructor in the airmen's school. Of course I happily agreed to his proposal, not even inquiring about the details. He added that he would confirm everything that day in a telegram he would send to me.

There was no limit to my satisfaction and self-esteem. I could share my joy, however, only with Yuri who had suffered no less than I. From our co-workers, even from those who had seemed very well disposed toward us, envy could well be detected. Although it was sad to realize this, I could well understand why. Obviously they felt somewhat humiliated by the type of work we were now managing to avoid. All of them belonged to the European intelligentsia and it was somewhat demeaning for them to get stuck for a long time doing menial work.

This was the only unpleasantness that went with our good fortune. I had to leave alone and prepare for Yuri's arrival. The Kochubeys were very nice and allowed Yuri to live with them until I could get established. In only a few days I was en route to my new position.

# 7

# LIFE IN AMERICA AND EUROPE

## *SYRACUSE*

At Syracuse I became acquainted with my teacher colleagues and students, who for the most part, had already finished college and were ranked among either lieutenants or colonels.

A Latvian headed my group and my old friend from Germany, Jaworksy, was also teaching in it. Each teacher taught five days a week, five hours a day. Usually, each instructor had his own group although, at times we would switch in order for the students to get used to various pronunciations and to a different voice, male and female.

I was so satisfied with my work that I plunged into it wholeheartedly. It was such a great and pleasant change in my fortune! From the students in my group I especially recall a Captain Stevenson. Nature had been very generous to him; he was tall, handsome, full of life, extremely cordial, both with his student friends and with the instructors. Everybody loved him. His nice wife and charming daughter, Connie (who immediately became my favorite), complete the picture. The Stevensons often invited us over for the evening. I made records for him in Russian so that he could listen to them at home after classes and thus, get more practice with Russian pronunciation. (I never lost touch with the Stevenson family. Every year we exchange at least one letter or postcard and in 1957 I visited them in London; in 1967 he and Connie came to visit me in Los Angeles where I was giving a lecture at U.C.L.A. We met again in 1977 when I taught a summer semester in Oregon, and we met the last time in 1979 in Seattle when Stevenson, with his son and charming daughter, my favorite Connie, came to the airport to see me. And this year, 1983, I just phoned him to tell him I was writing my memoirs.)

There were many other very nice people about whom I have retained the fondest memories; but, alas, contact has long since been lost. I still remember one student of Polish origin, not so much because of his talent in the Russian language but because of his charming three-year-old son. This boy never could get used to my Russian accent and to my limited English. He would keep repeating to me that I said everything very strangely and that I should learn from him.

There was another fine student, Pletcher, with whom fate reunited us after a twenty nine year separation. In 1979, when I flew to Seattle, I was supposed to have a three hour layover in Denver, where Pletcher was living. Stevenson, who was taking me to the airport, and who was still maintaining friendly relations with his former classmate, decided to inform Pletcher by telephone that I would be coming to Denver.

Pletcher came immediately to the airport and greeted everyone arriving on the plane. He was certain that he would recognize me immediately. But, alas! After twenty nine years this was not so easy. We did not meet each other. When I returned to Iowa, he phoned me and we talked for a long time. We later exchanged letters and photos—so as to avoid any future misadventures. Soon thereafter he moved to Florida and from there sent me photos of his family, three handsome, grown sons who reminded me of that young lieutenant I had known twenty-nine years ago.

Also in my memory are two students, Hall and Svob—both quite tall, cheerful, and very nice, who loved to go to New York on weekends. They often invited me to go along with them and en route we would converse for six hours only in Russian; this helped them more than an entire week in class. (In 1980, traveling through America with a friend who had come to visit from Germany, I stopped at Reno and phoned Svob. I was shocked to hear from his father that he had an incurable brain tumor and had already been hospitalized for several months.)

Yuri entered school in Syracuse and our daily routine became established. He soon was accepted into the chess club and began to participate in tournaments. My joy knew no limits when he won one of these tournaments.

My work in the school went very well and my relationship with the students was wonderful. Discipline was always maintained by the senior officer in the group, and, in spite of my pitiful knowledge of English, there were never any difficulties.

I remember an incident one day with one young teacher who was supposed to conduct the class with my favorite section. Obviously it was the day the two of us exchanged groups. The young teacher was waiting for me in the corridor completely confused and extremely uneasy. When I asked him what he was doing there and why was he not going to class, he answered that the students were playing cards with such enthusiasm that they paid absolutely no attention to him.

He was unable to restore order. This seemed very funny to me, and I returned with him. Knowing me as their teacher, the students immediately put down their cards; and the frightened young man whom the students had never before seen, and whom they had not accepted as a teacher because of his youth, was able to conduct his lesson in peace.

With the coming of summer, a great joy for me was the unexpected move of Varya to an estate near Syracuse. She was continuing to work as a servant for rich Americans, and they even allowed her to receive guests. Since Varya had no one except Yuri and me, when we didn't go to New York we tried to spend those free days with her in the lap of nature in that beautiful estate on the shores of the lake.

Graduation was approaching and I sadly thought how it would be to be separated from all these nice young men with whom I had been working for eleven months. I thought about the possibility that we would never see each other again. America is such a huge country and they would be going off in all directions.

Again I involuntarily thought about Russia. People there were far less mobile. This was especially true of people who lived, as we had, in Leningrad. All friends and acquaintances had lived for centuries it seems in that very same place. There one was not even permitted to move from one city to another except for important reasons, and nobody even tried to move. Those with whom one had been friends early in life remained one's friends until the end. The relationships between people were closer.

In America, however, the mobility always amazes me. I cannot get used to it. Some of the students, especially those with a family, even buy homes knowing that in a year they will have to move and, consequently, will have to sell the house and go to their new assignment.

Soon a rumor began circulating that a new professor was coming with the assignment to write a book by which we would be teaching. This was very odd for if the book had not been written, how were we supposed to begin teaching from it?

However, our job was not to judge that. The new group of 100 students was supposed to be experimental. Against my wishes, but as a great honor from the point of view of the administration, I was transferred to this group.

When all these 100 students appeared in the huge hall where the director was supposed to introduce us to them, I immediately noticed one cheerful, nice-looking, pleasant, young fellow, spouting off Russian proverbs.

Before the official part of the program I was able to talk with him and found out that he was from Chicago, and his name was Marshall. To my question of where had he learned so many proverbs, he answered with a laugh that his hobby was collecting proverbs and saying them. It turned out he had more than one hundred in his notebook. A few days later my Marshall got me into hot water with one of the teachers by going up to her and saying, "This dress suits you like a saddle on a cow." Seeing that I had often conversed with him, she of course suspected that I had put him up to it after teaching him that saying.

Genuine friendships were made with some of these students. Unfortunately, with the passage of so many years, contact has been lost with several. However, a few remained faithful friends and we correspond and sometimes even meet. I very much cherish these long friendships and, when I am at home in Iowa, the telephone might ring and an unfamiliar voice say, "Do you remember me, I was your student in Syracuse thirty years ago." It raises my spirits immensely, and I am happy and thankful that even in our materialistic century there still exists something far more valuable than money and earthly goods.

Incidentally, while I worked in this program, the director several times warned us teachers about the secrecy of our work, and that should anyone ask us about it, we were to answer that we were teachers at Syracuse University. Under no circumstances were we to mention our military school. Frightened by this, we did not even tell our relatives!

How great was our amazement when one of the teachers, opening the Soviet newspaper *Pravda,* read a long article with all the details about our program and with a complete list of the instructors, the traitors of the motherland.

Again we had to recognize that Soviet intelligence was everywhere and they had their way of finding out what interested them. We translated this article and sent it to the director.

When the position at the Syracuse Language School came to an end, I again had to look for a job. My student Spencer suggested I go with him to visit his relatives in Boston and stop en route at various colleges and universities in the hope of finding a teaching position. Nothing came of these efforts, however. All of these places demanded American degrees and paid no attention to Russian diplomas, even though on mine it was indicated I had received twelve excellents out of thirteen grades. It was some consolation that we visited many interesting places including the charming city of Boston and had become acquainted with many people.

Taking leave of Spencer, who was just as disappointed as I at my failure to find a position, I headed for Washington with letters of recommendation for Jakobson, who had an important position in the Library of Congress. His wife of many years was a professor of Russian at George Washington University. I was very well received; however, there was no hope for any employment there. I returned to Syracuse and with Varya, who had also settled there, began to look for housework. At this time another Russian family, the Giatsintovs, arrived in Syracuse. Their son Kolya was just about the same age as Yuri, and they became very good and lasting friends.

Late in August I began work in a student restaurant where I stayed out of necessity for five years. I should like to cross this period out of memory; but, again, even here under the very most difficult of circumstances there were bright and happy moments, always connected with people. This time these people were the American students whom we served. Often they were very low on funds. Our restaurant was distinguished for its Russian pastries, and we would manage to slip them an extra piece of the very tasty rum cake, out of sight of the watchful restaurant owner. On Sundays, when all the other student cafeterias were closed, crowds of students would descend on ours, so that it was always difficult to get a seat.

In that restaurant Yuri, Kolya, and many other girls and boys from the Russian emigre families were working several hours a day. These Russian families had settled in Syracuse mainly because of the school for airmen. Now many of the older generation were out of work; the children were looking for any type of earnings and willingly went to work in the restaurant where I had to take emloyment.

The Soviet launching in 1957 of Sputnik changed my entire life. I was accepted into the university graduate college on the basis of my Leningrad documents and was even given a stipend. I entered the Department of Comparative Literature to work toward a doctorate, as my work at Leningrad was accepted as an M.A. equivalent. Although I had to sit in class next to students far younger, I was not distressed; just the opposite. I considered myself a most fortunate person. The stipend sufficed for everything essential that Yuri and I needed. We lived very modestly and were completely satisfied with this turn of events. It seemed that fortune had again smiled upon us.

### MY ACQUAINTANCE WITH MARCEL AIMÉ

The English language was still a problem. However, my professors allowed me to present the assignments in French. Even the discussions of my papers in class were conducted in French. This lightened my work tremendously. My professors and colleagues—there were only five others in my class—were very favorably disposed toward me.

I still remember as though it were yesterday the anxiety with which I handed my professor of nineteenth-century French literature, Professor Bart, my first written work, a term paper about Stendahl. This was something we had never had to do in the Soviet Union. Indeed, almost all the exams there were oral, and the written work of an entirely different nature.

I can scarcely describe my amazement and joy when the professor returned my work with the grad A-. Indeed, this was one of the happiest moments of my life. This gave me confidence and the assurance that I could do the work to get this essential doctoral degree, something that had heretofore seemed insurmountable. I already knew that without my doctorate, I could not work at any American university.

I blessed Professor Bart, for he had saved me with his evaluation. Another person to whom I was especially indebted in that period of my studies at Syracuse was Professor Menu, that very same man who had hired me at the airforce school, where he had been the program director. Professor Menu gave a course on twentieth-century literature. I prepared long reports, in French, for him—even more than were demanded of me. A connoisseur of Russian literature, Professor Menu often dwelled on Russian writers during his discussions of my assignments. This made the debates and discussion livelier and easier.

I passed the first and second semesters with great results and I was accepted into the Honor Society of Phi Sigma Iota. Now it was necessary to think about a dissertation. Completely by accident I came upon the name of a French writer, Marcel Aimé, whose works I had especially liked. Even more, he seemed to me to be an extraordinary person.

I did not stop to think about this very long but decided to write and tell him I was preparing to write a dissertation about him. An answer came by return mail. His letter was extremely kind and very encouraging. I showed it to all my professors, who were quite impressed. All of them, especially Menu, were very satisfied with this turn of events. The contact with the writer about whom I was preparing to write was an investment in my future success.

And thus, in the spring of 1959, began my correspondence with this outstanding writer and person. My subsequent meeting and acquaintanceship with him had a great influence in the years to come.

Yuri, meanwhile, had finished high school and entered college. Dima, whose place of residence was New York went to Germany to finish medical school.

In Syracuse there was a large Russian colony and two Russian churches. There were evening parties, even balls; Christmas, the New Year, and Easter were celebrated. Yuri had a great number of friends among the young people but, nonetheless, his best friend remained Kolya Giatsintov about whose arrival in Syracuse I have already spoken.

I finished all my course work in 1960; there remained the final exam and the thesis defense. Since I could no longer hope for a renewal of the stipend, which I had been receiving for two years, I had to think about looking for a job for the next academic year, and try to pass the exams in the fall. I felt it was essential to get acquainted with Marcel Aimé before then so that I would be able to give my advisor the first chapters of my dissertation. From Marcel Aimé, the original source, I could get all essential information. This was extremely important.

While I was preparing to go to Paris, I sent out several requests for employment to different universities that were seeking a professor of Russian.

During the previous year, my professor of French literature had been a very nice young man of Greek origin, Christofatis, who had spent three years at the University of Iowa. In a conversation about my plans for the future, he advised me to write to Iowa and offer my services as a professor of Russian language and literature. I was very doubtful about being accepted, since I still had not finished my doctorate and could not count on getting an assistant professorship. Nonetheless, influenced by Christofatis, I wrote to the University of Iowa.

At that time Iowa seemed to be an extremely distant and terribly remote spot on the world map. To my great surprise, very soon after I sent my letter, I received a phone call from the head of the Department of Foreign Languages, Dr. de Chasca. He offered me a position beginning in the fall as an instructor, since I had not yet completed my dissertation. In addition, he wanted me to come for an interview in the middle of May. Gathering my courage (for I had no definite offer), I answered that I would not come for an interview since I already had my ticket for Paris on the 13th of May; also, I could not come as an instructor.

He answered that in that case, he would have to speak with the dean, and then he would let me know. After the conversation I was somewhat downcast and shared my feelings with Yuri. I was afraid I had lost out and that I would have to find something else since my stipend was running out and we had no other resources. Yuri's inexhaustible optimism was an immense support in this anxious and important time.

Three other applications to universities in Reno, California, and Columbia, remained unanswered for the time being. Of these three possible positions, I was most attracted by Nevada, since my former student, Svob, lived and worked in Reno. He spoke with me on the telephone and strongly persuaded me to come to Reno, promising to help in every way.

I spent two anxious days cursing myself for my self-confidence and my self-confident tone in the conversation with Professor de Chasca, a tone that was in no way consistent with my character.

There was no limit to my surprise and joy when on May 9, 1960 I received a telegram with the following message, "You have been appointed Assistant Professor with a salary of $6,500 a year as of September of this year." Signed "de Chasca—head of the Department of Foreign Languages." Several days later I received the contract. Thus, Yuri's and my fate had been decided.

A few days later came two other answers: one from Reno, the other from Columbia. I wrote them that I had accepted an offer from Iowa. The 1960s were the most favorable period for teachers of Russian seeking employment.

In celebration, I divided with Yuri that money which still remained from my work at the Kochubeys, and on the 13th of May we left for Europe. I went by air and Yuri by ship to Amsterdam.

### SUMMER IN EUROPE

I arrived in Paris early on the morning of the 14th and was met there by my niece Tanya whom I had not seen for such a long time. She and her husband, a French army colonel, lived in a suburb. My spirits were high and absolutely everything delighted me; meeting relatives, the wonderful Parisian spring, and, most important of all, the knowledge that I had definite work beginning in the fall. All my cares were forgotten. The future no longer worried me.

A salary of $6,500 seemed to be unbelievable riches in comparison with the stipend of $1,500 I had received for two years and, even more, in comparison with the previous pay in America for work in the hotels and restaurants. I did not look closely at the contract from Iowa, in which it was stated that I had been hired on a probationary basis for one year only.

Shortly after my arrival in Paris I phoned Marcel Aimé. His wife answered the phone and I told her that the relatives with whom I was staying unfortunately had no phone. I therefore gave her their address. I then waited for a message from Marcel Aimé. I did not for a minute doubt that he would answer, especially since I had received all those exceptional letters from him while in Syracuse.

However, time passed and I heard not a word from him. My spirits sank. Tanya suggested that we go for a week to a Russian pension in the Loire castle region. I agreed. The charming castles and the stay in a pleasant guest house among nice people distracted me from the injured feelings I sustained when Marcel Aimé had not responded to my desire to meet him.

Once, completely by chance in a small village on the Loire, we met the French critic Catelin, who had written a good book about the works of Marcel Aimé. This critic, a rather eccentric young man, on hearing who I was, came up to me and reproachfully asked where had I gone, why had I not let Marcel Aimé know that I was leaving Paris? Marcel Aimé had been searching for me for two weeks and had lost hope of locating me. The misunderstanding was soon cleared up.

His wife had made an error when noting my address; and although an invitation for dinner had been sent to me, I had obviously not received it. They had waited for me for a long time that evening, until finally Marcel Aimé had taken his car and driven to the address given him by his wife. Of course he was unable to find me. I was both happy and in despair, because I had involuntarily caused such a problem and not shown up for that formal dinner.

Fortunately for me everything turned out fine. I wrote Aimé, explaining the misunderstanding. He invited me to a Danish restaurant in the Champs-Elysées. The evening spent in this elegant restaurant remained in my memory for a long time. I was in a wonderful mood. To be with this famous French writer in such a restaurant, where many persons knew him, and to have the possibility of speaking with him simply and at ease cheered me immeasurably.

The next day there was another happy occurrence. I met Yuri at the station. He had arrived from Amsterdam and he too was in a very good mood, having spent a number of days on the boat in the happy company of other students. He wanted to spend several days exploring Paris and then buy a used motorcycle and travel around Europe. Back in America my former student, Bill Spencer, had told us he too was planning to visit Paris at the same time.

I found a room for both of them in a pension not far from the relatives with whom I was living. Back then it was quite easy for American students to travel in Europe, and the exchange rate was very favorable. In many cities there were student dormitories where they could spend the night and receive breakfast for virtually nothing. In Germany, for example, the dollar bought 4 marks and 20 pfennig, and a night's lodging cost only 1 mark—or less than 25¢. In France the exchange rate was even more favorable. With such rates of exchange, Yuri and I considered ourselves millionaires. Everything in life is, of course, relative. But for us, in comparison with the past, everything seemed so easy and attainable.

Yuri, who always took a strong personal interest in all my affairs, was ecstatic when I told him about my dinner with Marcel Aimé.

After a few days spent together in Paris, since Bill had unfortunately not found us in Paris, having misplaced the address, Yuri bought a used motorcycle for $30, a motorcycle that roared unmercifully, and left for his trip. I reserved a room in a pension for $8, everything included, in Bad Kissingen, Germany, and at the beginning of July left Paris. I had to prepare seriously for my fall exams and I felt that this modest pension in a German spa was an ideal place for this.

I was not mistaken, I had a large bright room with all the conveniences, most of all, a fine, large desk, something that one does not always find in European spas. Getting up every day between five and six o'clock in the morning, I worked diligently until 9:30. Then I would go to breakfast. Afterward I would walk a lot, often meeting the most interesting people. Then, from three until supper, I would again work in my room.

Soon Yuri came to visit me, after having traveled through France and visited our old friend Valya in Marseille. Valya had lived in Bendorf both during and after the war. It was during the French occupation of Germany that she had married a French officer and gone with him to the South of France.

Yuri liked Bad Kissingen so much that he remained there for two weeks. The owner of the guesthouse agreed to put a couch in my room and for $4 (18 marks) extra, Yuri would receive the same food as I. This was one of the most pleasant periods of both our lives. For Yuri, there was tennis, and there were walks in search of mushrooms for us both. It is true my studies suffered somewhat; but, nonetheless, I found time for everything.

In Bad Kissingen there was a Russian Church with the dearest old priest and his wife. Yuri and I visited him frequently. Once during the evening service, I noticed a pretty young woman who seemed to be visiting an Orthodox Church for the first time and did not know either the service or the ritual. I went to help her; and, immediately after the service, we became acquainted and began conversing. She was a Russian from Poltava who had come to Germany during the war. Her husband was a German that by some whim of fate, had been able to get her out of a camp for those returning to the Soviet motherland. Somehow he had managed to distract the guards and, putting Anushka on his motorcycle, had brought her to his home town, Siegen, where she is living today.

That evening she came to see us, and we became almost inseparable. From the beginning, Anushka adored Yuri. This, of course, endeared her all the more to me. Pretty, nice, and cheerful, she made a good impression on everyone. Yuri soon left to continue his European travels. Anushka, however, remained my true companion.

Yuri and I agreed to meet in Karlsruhe, where our Leningrad acquaintances, the Davidenkovs, were living. After Karlsruhe, we intended to go to Switzerland where we also had nice acquaintances whom we had met by chance on the train, and who were insisting we visit them.

The Black Forest, Switzerland, Paris again, all flashed by like a bright dream. I had to return for the doctoral exams, and Yuri had to get back for the beginning of the school term. I arrived in Syracuse the 1st of September 1960 and the next day began writing four hours a day on the exams that had been prepared for me. This continued for an entire week.

The 22nd of September, the day after Yuri's return, Nadine, a young French girl, arrived. She was the daughter of my old friends, the Chomets. I had met them that year in Paris and when they asked me to take Nadine, who wanted very much to see America, I agreed. I did not mention that after my trip I only had $400 and if everything went perfectly well I would receive my first pay only after a month of work. I very willingly agreed to have this young French girl live with me during the time of her stay in the United States. Of course, I also did not mention that I still had no apartment in my new city and not the faintest idea of how and when I would get set up there.

En route from Syracuse to Iowa, I had many good acquaintances so it was not necessary to stay at hotels or motels. The first stage, with a stop at Niagara Falls, ended late in the evening in Cleveland at the home of friends from Piatigorsk, the Mironenkos. These friends put on a big party in our honor. On the one hand, such attention was very nice; however, it was very out of place since Nadine and I were very tired after such a long trip and wanted to sleep. The next day we had another long trip ahead of us—to Chicago where a former student from the airforce school, Marshall, the devotee of Russian sayings and proverbs, was awaiting us. It was a wonderful meeting. Marshall came running to the phone booth with a bottle of champagne in his hands. We had become hopelessly lost in the Chicago traffic.

The next morning we drove the last short leg of our journey to Iowa. When the road sign indicating Iowa City flashed before my eyes, my heart was seized with excitement. What awaited me in this new, unfamiliar, and distant place? I was very glad that I was not alone and had with me this young person, full of life and hope for a happy future. Her optimism encouraged me. I thought it was a good thing that I agreed when her parents asked and had taken Nadine with me! Somehow, everything would work out fine. The worst and most difficult times were behind me.

We went straight to the Hotel Jefferson, where Professor de Chasca had reserved a room for us. Nadine was delighted by everything, from the small restaurants where we had stopped, to the large, well-furnished hotel room. However, I saw the card on the doors with the price—$10 a night. That seemed to me an exceptionally high price.

*IOWA*

I decided that as of the morning I would use all of my efforts to find ourselves an apartment. By now my reserves had pretty much melted away on the trip, despite a number of favorable circumstances, such as free lodging and gas wars in several states. In Iowa, for example, the price of a gallon of gas had dipped to 17¢, compared with the usual price at that time of 30¢.

It seems, however, that at the most difficult moments of my life, fate somehow takes care of me. Not telling Nadine anything of my worries, I calmly went to bed and immediately fell asleep.

The next day was the beginning of registration. Having no idea of where and how this registration was handled, I went to the dean's office. He was not there but I saw his secretary, Mary Lou Kelley, who turned out to be a cordial, very sweet person and explained everything to me. Mr. de Chasca was also at registration. I immediately headed there, asking him for permission to use the day to find a place to live.

When I returned to the hotel I took a chance and paid the bill, not reserving the room for the night. Nadine and I then set out to look for an apartment. This was no easy matter. The students had long since looked over the place and rented the apartments that were close to the university.

We looked everywhere, inquiring even of the passersby if they knew of vacancies. At two o'clock I bought the paper that had just come out and by four o'clock I had rented what seemed to us a very nice apartment. It was right across from the cemetary on Church Street. The nearness of the cemetary in no way bothered us. The quiet was calming and we had no superstitions about nocturnal visits from the deceased.

Unpacking our small amount of luggage did not take long. All my possessions had easily fitted into the trunk of my Pontiac. Nadine and I decided we had been lucky.

After paying a month's rent of $75 in advance, I was left with the large balance of capital totalling $200. This had to last for a month until we received our first pay. I went to buy groceries in the very best of spirits.

The next day, not knowing where I could park the car, Nadine dropped me off at the Field House where registration was taking place.

Everything was new for me. I was especially uneasy because of the enormous amount of mail awaiting me. A Russian Department, as such, did not yet exist. All the foreign language departments, except the German, were under de Chasca. I was the only Russian professor. In addition to me there were three assistants, Tamara, a Russian; Zuleika, a Serbian; and Oreste, a Western Ukrainian.

Many students had enrolled for Russian. I already knew from correspondence with de Chasca that I had to teach the second, third, and fourth courses of Russian. In addition, there was a course in technical Russian and an evening course for the military reserves. Whether or not I was obliged to do the latter I did not yet know. In addition, all the clerical work of the Russian department, especially the correspondence, fell to me.

Nadine was no bother to me whatsoever. On the contrary, she helped me in any way she could. The students and residents of the city were captivated both by her attractive appearance and by her language. She spoke English quite well but with an amusing French accent.

Dean Stuit put on a dinner in the Union for all the newly appointed instructors. My neighbor at this dinner was President Hancher, who conversed at great length with me and asked me many questions about Russia and our experiences.

During the first days of our arrival, Mary Lou Kelley and her sister Alice invited us on a trip around the city and its surroundings. Both of us liked Iowa very much. This state reminded me of Russia, especially of the Ukraine. Within a week of our arrival, we put on a gala dinner.

Our first guests were the Kelley sisters, both of whom had been extremely nice to us since our arrival and shown us many favors. Their cordial assistance laid the foundation for our new life in Iowa. We knew that here too we would have true friends and helpers.

I was usually busy until two. At two o'clock Nadine would come for me and we would go back to our apartment. I still had to finish my dissertation; therefore, if I had not become too tired in the morning, I would work a few hours at home. Once a week we would make a point of visiting all the neighboring colleges in order to get acquainted with the Russian language teachers. It seemed essential to me to have contact with my colleagues.

In Cedar Rapids at Coe College, a young Serb, Batinic, was teaching Russian. His wife was French; this was nice not only for me but especially for Nadine. We also became friends with a very pleasant and cultured couple, the Michailoviches. He was a professor of Russian, she of German and French, at Cornell College in Mt. Vernon.

Nadine loved to drive the car. I was happy to allow her this pleasure. We tried to get to know the region where we would be living and drove around the area. I liked Iowa more each day.

Yuri had remained at the University of Syracuse where he was studying chemistry. I was sorry that he was not in Iowa and, for the time being, was secretly dreaming of getting him to come to Iowa. I could in no way get used to the fact that in America the majority of children leave the parental house after high school and lead an independent life. I could not forget Russia where even adult children, studying in college, remained under the parental roof. It is difficult to say which is better, but in Russia family ties are somehow stronger. Until now, Yuri and I had never been separated for long. Now I was suffering greatly from our separation.

How often I thanked fortune that I was not alone and that I had not been afraid to take Nadine. She distracted and entertained me in so many ways. Being very pretty, which I have already mentioned, and having a fine French wit, she attracted to our apartment both young students charmed by her and older persons who wished to visit us. Three weeks later we again put on a Franco-Russian dinner and invited, besides the Kelleys, Dr. de Chasca and his wife. Soon our dinners became commonplace and we were happy with our guests' delight in our culinary inventions.

I was very satisfied with my students. I felt they had accepted me with open hearts and were studying hard and becoming interested in all things Russian. In our department I was totally independent. Mr. de Chasca did not mix into the details of my work, giving me complete freedom. This made my work very satisfying.

He indeed knew how to create a very pleasant atmosphere for all his subordinates. I felt this especially strongly in comparison with my previous employment in the Soviet Union, in Hitler Germany, and even in my subordination to some arrogant French officers during the period of French occupation. This beginning under de Chasca laid a good foundation for my happy life both in the university and in the state of Iowa.

October and a large part of November flew past quickly. Nadine and I already had many acquaintances who regularly visited us and tried to get us involved in the life of the university and the city.

That year we became acquainted with a French girl, Françoise, who had received her degree from our university. In Paris she had become acquainted with actress Jean Seberg from Marshalltown, Iowa and had been advised to choose Iowa of the two or three offers she had received. Françoise resembled Jean very much and when she went to visit Jean's parents, one of Jean's former suitors was on the street and rushed toward her. He was certain that Jean had returned home. After this trip by Françoise to Marshalltown, an article appeared in the local newspaper with her photo alongside that of Jean.

Among Nadine's many admirers one especially stood out. She had become acquainted with him by chance. A medical student who had been going out with Françoise, Steve Walsh, arranged a blind date for Nadine with his friend, Larry Severeid, also a medical student. Nadine's heart was taken from the very first day by this handsome lad. She started to go out with Larry every Friday and Saturday. Sometimes in the middle of the week he would invite her out in the evening for a cup of coffee, while taking a break from his studies. Nadine always awaited his invitations anxiously.

When she would return after the evening spent with Larry, she would ask me to listen to all the details of the evening they had spent and under no circumstances could I fall asleep before she had finished. Sometimes she would detain me till one or two in the morning. Immediately upon returning she would rush to me, sit down by my bed, and begin telling me all about her evening's adventures. I, however, was fighting against the drowsiness that was overpowering me; and I would have to force my heavy eyes to stay open while listening to her ecstatic tales. Woe to me if I would fall alseep before the end of her story. I would not be forgiven. Nadine would be angry with me the entire next day. But since I was her only trusted friend, she would control her anger and forgive me and, the next time, would continue to entrust her secrets to me. I would try to be a more attentive listener.

Thanksgiving Day we spent at the Kelley sisters', where there was a gala dinner at which their brother, with his wife and son, were also present. Their son Carter, the owner of a magnificent car, offered to take Nadine on a ride around the outskirts of the city. However, Nadine was in love with Larry and Carter made little impression on her.

The next day, rising early in the morning, I looked out the window and was cheered by the beautiful, sunny, cloudless day. The thought occurred to me to go somewhere further than the outskirts of Iowa City where we always drove. Nadine was sleeping soundly when I awakened her with the suggestion, "Let's drive south, at least as far as St. Louis." I did not have to say it twice; she was up imediately and rushing me. In about half an hour we were already en route toward Missouri. Previously, one of our acquaintances had told us that there was much of interest in St. Louis, mainly a magnificent bridge. We had neither map nor brochures with descriptions of the city. We simply decided that we would stop and ask pedestrians for suggestions, but unfortunately they had no idea what would be of interest to us. At that time I saw two policemen standing on the corner and talking. We drove up and asked whether they knew of anything worthwhile seeing in town. This unexpected question, apparently, intrigued the young men. They were interested in knowing who we were. I satisfied their curiosity by telling them that I was Russian and Nadine was French, having just come from Paris. After talking it over, the policemen announced, "We aren't working today. If you want to follow us, we'll show you our city." Very satisfied with the turn of events, we followed our guides.

This trip, lasting more than two hours, was a great adventure for us. The policemen stopped before every point of interest and took turns getting out of the car, coming over to us, and explaining everything. Often a whole line of cars would form behind us, not having the faintest idea of what was happening. To honk at or pass police cars was, apparently, not allowed. While I was hurrying after our new guides, afraid to lose them, I ran a red light. I noticed with horror that the sheriff himself was following right behind me. Fortunately for us our new friends, also taking note of our unwelcome witness, jumped out of their car and approached us. This apparently satisfied the guardian of order who drove on.

The last stop was the shore of the Missouri. Ships were anchored in the river, and there we took a number of photos. It was already rather late and I proposed to our guides that we take them to a restaurant. It was very interesting to look at the people in the restaurant and see their faces when we appeared. Our young, elegant Nadine and I, escorted by two armed, uniformed policemen. We walked freely into the restaurant and sat down at a table. One or another of the guests were constantly glancing at us; this I found highly amusing. After dinner our guides led us to the road to Iowa City; and we arrived home late at night, very tired but very content.

We were visiting the Kelleys when, for the first time in our lives, we saw a presidential election on television. As is known, Kennedy won. We personally felt neither delight nor sadness. All of this was quite strange for me. The preceding elections of Eisenhower had passed completely unnoticed by me. At that time I was unable to vote, and all the political events had somehow slid past unnoticed.

At the beginning of December of that very same 1960, I began to experience strong pains in the area of my stomach. On December 5, I went to the doctor. A series of tests showed I was suffering from gall stones and that I needed an operation right away. I was in despair. How would it all turn out? Indeed, I had just begun to work, and suddenly I would have to be in the hospital for a long period of time. Vacation would begin the 16th. I decided to go to the hospital on the 13th, thinking that I would be absent from work only three days and that my assistants could replace me. This I did. Nadine took me to the hospital on the 13th.

In the ward there was an extremely nice woman from West Liberty who took me under her protection and acquainted me with all the rules of an American hospital. This was very pleasant for me, and I awaited the terrible day without fear.

The operation was long and difficult. When I finally came to after the anesthesia, my whole body was aching and it seemed to me that I would not be able to endure these pains. In the corner of the ward I saw Nadine's small figure. It was such an unimaginable comfort to know that one of your own was nearby. I felt that she really was concerned about me. I remember that I said only one thing; "Nadine, it's terrible."

Some special apparatus was set up to feed me through my veins. Something else was put in my throat which prevented me from speaking and I could only make a few sounds. Toward night Françoise came. Both girls requested permission from my surgeon, Dr. Geiss, to remain with me the whole night. My girls were afraid I would not survive. In addition, the machine, which they had never seen before, frightened them.

The night was a complete nightmare. There was oppressive pain, insomnia, melancholy, fear of the future, and the feeling that I would never recover. I would just begin to doze off when my two "nurses" would rush toward me, thinking that I was already departing from this world. Of course I would be immediately awakened and instead start tossing around. They would constantly run to the senior nurse, assuring her that the interveinous liquid food was running out and that I would die. As a result of this, the hospital had had enough and the doctor refused them permission to remain there the following night, something they had again requested.

At that time, I couldn't fully appreciate their efforts. Nor did I know that Françoise was supposed to teach that whole day. This was not easy after a sleepless night. Now, however, after the passage of more than twenty years, I clearly and gratefully remember these two girls and their unselfishness and concern for me.

From the following day on, visitors were allowed into my room. There was no more space on the tables or around the bed for the flowers that had arrived. The room was a greenhouse. My surgeon, Dr. Geiss, could not get over the amount of attention I was getting from my students and colleagues, who had known me only three months. I, of course, was very happy and very touched. I believe that that is what speeded my recovery.

Yuri, who had been informed of my condition by the girls, arrived after a few days too. This was a great moral boost. Yuri brought a letter from Syracuse saying I had passed the exams and now only the dissertation remained.

Among my assistants, as I have already mentioned, was one young fellow—a Ukrainian, Orest Okhrimovich. I had thought he was not especially well-disposed toward me. He was always frowning and spoke little, and I had thought he was dissatisfied with my teaching. He had been a student in one of my classes and had never come to speak with me after class like the others. My illness and stay in the hospital changed everything. Orest was one of the first to come and bring beautiful flowers.

I could still scarcely speak but looked at him with thanks. He, however, told me about a similar illness his mother had had and tried to calm me by saying it was not as big a thing as it seemed. Since then, Orest and I became good friends and have met on a number of occasions even after he moved from our university to teach in Wisconsin. I always remember him with warmth.

During the first days of my difficult condition, my roommate was replaced by another. However, as often happens in my life, in misfortune there is luck. The new patient turned out to be just as nice as her predecessor.

She began to help me with absolutely everything. The question arose as to where I could go after I was dismissed from the hospital. Our apartment was on the second floor, and with its narrow, steep staircase, could scarcely serve as refuge after such a serious operation. Then fortune smiled. The Kelley sisters offered to have me come to their house until I had fully recovered.

Involuntarily I recalled my thoughts of almost ten years earlier, when Yuri and I had approached the Statue of Liberty on that memorable May evening. My heart had been heavy with worry about the unknown future and the fear of how the two of us, without knowing the language, without relatives or friends, would be able to make our way in this new country among a foreign people.

But even then, a deep faith in humanity brought me out of depression. Now I was convinced that I was not mistaken. Everywhere it is possible to meet people like the Kelleys. I had not only come across such people at home in Russia, but even among the enemy, the Germans; and among the French who were occupying Germany; and now here in America, which had seemed to me so distant and so strange.

On the 24th of December, Yuri took me to the Kelley's home.

Christmas Eve we spent with them, with their Christmas tree, gifts, and, most important of all, in a family atmosphere.

The French girls were not there. They had been invited to the Walsh's, in Ames. Françoise had been very attracted to Steve, a classmate of Larry Severeid, who had arranged for Larry to meet Nadine. Nadine had hoped that Larry would be in Ames and was already anticipating the holidays with pleasure.

Dima came to visit me the 26th of December. The Kelleys invited my sons for the holiday dinner. Three days later they both left. Dima had to return to work and Yuri wanted to spend New Year's Eve with his young Russian friends in Syracuse.

The girls returned earlier than they had expected. Nadine's hopes to meet Larry were not realized, and Françoise was somewhat put out by Steve's lack of attention. Despite a very cordial reception by Walsh's parents, they decided to hurry back home.

At the beginning of January, I was getting ready to move back to the apartment I shared with Nadine. However, my girls, after whispering back and forth with the Kelleys, began to try to persuade me to remain a few extra days. I regarded this as exploitation of hospitality and could not understand the reason for their stubborn desire not to take me home. I was so insistent that Nadine finally told me they had decided to put on a huge party in our apartment on the occasion of the orthodox Christmas, the 7th of January. I had to reconcile myself to this so as not to spoil their celebration.

When the Kelleys and I arrived on Church Street on the 7th, I could not believe my eyes. Our little apartment was overflowing. Guests were standing in the kitchen, the corridor, and almost in the bathroom. My assistants, Tamara and Zuleika, were there with their husbands; so was Orest with his girlfriend; some of my students; Kelley's nephew with a girlfriend; and some medical students, friends of Steve and Larry. Of course, the heroes of both of my French girls were there and had made themselves pretty much at home.

All the noise and bustle tired me. The Kelleys were reluctant to leave me there and took me home with them. I spent two extra days in their hospitable house; and, finally having recovered completely, I returned home and to my university duties. Nadine drove me every day by car. It was very difficult for me to go on foot, even though before my illness I had very much enjoyed taking walks. Nadine was a big help.

In February, one of the Russian students persuaded Nadine to go with other students to New Orleans during Mardi Gras. Two feelings were struggling in Nadine. On the one hand she wanted very much to see something new, especially colorful New Orleans and to drive through several states. On the other hand, she did not want to be separated from Larry, whose appeal to her I could easily judge from the stories after her evenings out with him. I said nothing, because it is difficult to advise in such cases.

One evening she asked me for the car and drove to Larry's, in order to get his agreement to this trip. She returned happy. It seems Larry did not object to her wish. The next day she, a girlfriend, and three students, left Iowa. The local paper even published a photo of my French girl by the car with the happy group around her. They left and everything got very quiet.

The university, the work on the dissertation, and the visits of lonely Françoise were my distractions during the next ten days, for the trip stretched out for more than the intended week.

Finally, one gray February day, the door to our apartment flew open and a beaming Nadine stood at the door with a thousand tales to tell. Until evening she was babbling. But, after a call to Larry, everything changed. She did not say a word, but disappeared and returned in two hours.

Since, because of her expansive nature she was unable to hide her feelings, that evening I was informed of the drama which had arisen. Larry had been against her trip, and this she had not mentioned. Now, however, in view of the length of the trip and her excitement, he suspected a romance. The conversation had not been too pleasant, and Larry refused to go with her that evening. There was nothing left for her to do but return home.

From that day on, there was a continuing series of tragedies in the life of my French girl. The main one, however, was the annual ball, put on by the med students. She had been sure she would be invited by her suitor. Great was her disappointment when no invitation came. On the evening of the ball, in despair—she had earlier prepared a charming outfit—she decided to implore Chuck Plummer, one of my students, to get a ticket and go with her. This was not such a brilliant idea. Immediately upon entering the large Union ballroom, where the dance was to take place, she came up against Larry in the company of a girl Nadine had never seen and who, alas, was very pretty. Seeing Nadine, Larry, apparently angered at meeting her there, left with his new girlfriend. Nadine and Chuck stayed there for some time, but by twelve o'clock she was sitting on my bed, tearfully telling me about what had occurred.

Suffering, Nadine lost all interest in Iowa life. She stopped going out in the evenings. Often she would cry bitterly on my shoulder, reproaching herself for her hair-brained idea of traveling with the group to Louisiana. She did not care for any of the boys who had gone with her on that trip and subsequently rejected all their attempts to invite her to parties, to the movies, or for coffee. Nobody could, even in part, replace Larry. He, however, had stopped phoning her.

During spring vacation, which coincided with the Orthodox Easter, I suggested to both French girls that we take a trip to Colorado. We left on Friday and returned Sunday, a week later. A collage of new impressions, beautiful places, meetings with various persons, had distracted them both. Nadine's former love of life had returned. She was especially enraptured by the "Garden of the Gods." The unusually beautiful rocks of magnificent shape impressed us all. We took many photos.

April flew by virtually unnoticed; and in May, after talking it over with my students who had driven to the West, Nadine began to prepare for the long trip with them through America.

At the beginning of June, I was supposed to fly to Paris, France for a second meeting with Marcel Aimé and further work on my dissertation, which I was preparing to defend no later than the beginning of 1962.

### PARIS, 1961

On the 8th of July, my niece Tanya and her husband were awaiting me in Paris. We would go together to Florence where they were planning to spend the month. Even before leaving for Italy, I phoned Marcel Aimé and was invited for dinner at his home. Again it was very pleasant to meet with him, to speak with such a dear and cultured person, and to sit in his study where so many famous works had been written.

We soon left for Florence, and I was seeing it for the first time. Every day we visited museums and exhibits and roamed through the streets where at every step something of interest was to be seen. The weather was fantastic.

At this time Yuri was in Europe with his friend Kolya Giatsintov and some other students. They were travelling in the car Kolya's older brother had had them buy for him. After travelling through Europe, they were to bring it to the United States. Yuri wrote that he was coming to visit me in Italy.

I was impatiently waiting for him, but he didn't arrive. We left Florence at the beginning of July, Tanya and her husband going to Paris. I again went to Bad Kissingen, to the same sanatorium where I had been the previous year. Yuri came there for a whole week, while his companions stayed in Yugoslavia at Kolya's relatives.

In September I returned to Iowa for the beginning of the semester. In the spring of 1961 the university administration had decided to hire a chairman for the Russian department to free de Chasca from an extremely burdensome load. A committee had been appointed to screen the applications of the many candidates who wanted to fill this position. Dr. de Chasca proposed a former student, Oppenheimer, who had received his doctorate in Spanish. I personally did not know any of the candidates and trusting the opinion of de Chasca, I also voted for Oppenheimer. Upon his arrival in the fall, I began to share my office with him. Our relations were good, and we didn't interfere with each other.

That year Bill Perkins, our famous football player, was one of my students. Perkins is a very interesting individual, and I should like to stop here for a bit in order to describe him. Bill is black, very handsome, tall and well-built, with beautiful, expressive eyes, and a flashing smile. He has a happy and easy-going personality, and the smile that almost never leaves his face is sincere and infectious. He was here on a four-year scholarship.

As my student, he brought me many happy moments; because of his easy-going and happy personality, he was able to cheer me up in moments of loneliness and sadness. But, my dear Perkins with his too easy-going ways at times created unnecessary excitement. At least, it added variety to my life. He was almost always late for class and when I would ask where he had been, he would explain with his charming smile that he couldn't find a place to park. Or he would come up with some other minor excuse. I scarcely believed him and suspected something else. He had great success with the ladies.

Nadine had returned to Paris after her trip through America, and Yuri was still in Syracuse. Françoise and I missed Yuri very much. We had agreed to live together that year and rented an unattractive apartment on Dubuque, next to the movie theater. Françoise was teaching and studying, so that she was rarely at home. I, however, after classes, would hurry home in order to finish retyping my dissertation.

Françoise, too, fell under Perkins' charm—and completely lost her head. She would even implore me to call him in the mornings, so that he would not be late for class, fearing that there might be unpleasantness for him if he overslept.

Our Russian circle met every week, first in one, then in another house. Françoise, not knowing a word of Russian, persistently attended the circle, only in order to meet her Perkins. But if he would meet her in the street by chance, and walk her home, she would be in ecstasy for the entire day. She even began to learn Russian phrases and would talk with Bill in a very amusing fashion.

To my lectures on Russian literature, Perkins would surreptiously bring a tape-recorder. He himself, however, lounging comfortably in the back rows, often would fall asleep. Once, seeing my football player peacefully sleeping, I awakened him with an unexpected question about Russian literature. To this question, I received a completely far-fetched and uncorresponding answer and the entire class laughed uproariously. Perkins, however, was in no way embarrassed by his "brilliant" answer. He just gave me a great, big smile.

That fall I often went to the football games and always looked for Number 81, Perkins. I was happy with his achievements on that front.

In February, 1962, Yuri transferred from Syracuse to our university, to the department of chemistry. I was extremely pleased with this. I soon found a room for him with a professor who rented rooms to students. For dinner, Yuri would come to us. He soon got to know all my students and preferred Bill. If I would correct notebooks and give Perkins a lower grade than the others, when Yuri was there he would argue with me, trying to prove that I was not fair and his friend Perkins had not written a worse paper than the others. Thus, Yuri, as well as Françoise, had become a true friend and champion of our famous Bill.

In March of this year we had an amusing incident in our apartment. Françoise and I had been asleep for quite a while when suddenly I saw a shadow between the kitchen and my room. I shouted to Françoise. The shadow immediately disappeared and I heard Françoise shouting at someone. Quickly getting dressed, I went out of the bedroom. Françoise began to tell me excitedly that someone had just been in the apartment.

Who, what and why were completely incomprehensible. He hadn't taken anything and apparently was completely confused himself. The assistant police chief lived right under us, and we were good acquaintances. Not wishing to awaken him, we telephoned the police station. Two armed policemen appeared immediately. They searched everything and found not a trace of our intruder.

I think they even believed we had imagined the whole thing. We were so agitated that we couldn't fall asleep the whole night. In the morning we went down to our policeman-neighbor's apartment and told him everything that had happened. He was surprised by our bravery to want to stay on in the apartment, and calmed us by his supposition of what had happened. Last year several coeds had lived in our apartment. Probably one of their boyfriends, who knew the room locations quite well, had climbed from the roof through the partially open window.

Apparently he was amazed to find foreigners there instead of his girlfriend. This version seemed most plausible to me.

Our Perkins, learning about the incident before anybody else, when he saw us smiled and asked Françoise without any hesitation, "Did you have a boyfriend at your place last night?"

Soon this misunderstanding was cleared up and the sheriff's suggestion turned out to be correct. One of my students told me that, indeed, one of the boyfriends of one of the girls who had lived there last year had climbed through the window.

This young fellow was no longer a student in our university and had arrived unexpectedly in Iowa. He had wanted to surprise his girlfriend with a nocturnal visit. I can just imagine what an unpleasant shock it was to come upon us. The incident was soon forgotten. Françoise became more careful and no longer left the window half-open. The assistant police chief tried to persuade us to move, but we stayed in that apartment until spring.

In the spring of 1962 I accepted an offer by Stilman, head of the Slavic department of Columbia University in New York, to teach in the summer program.

Yuri received summer work in the Chemistry Department at Iowa. He decided to take me by car to New York before school began. We left for New York with Pavel Batinic, who taught Russian at Coe College, and who had been divorced unexpectedly this spring. He wanted to go with us to look into possible job opportunities.

He was lucky. A week after our arrival a position opened up in the Columbia University summer program; and, on my recommendation, they hired Batinic for that position. At that time he was very cheerful, despite his divorce, and we got along very well.

In the summer session I had a huge class, about thirty students. At the very beginning of the course, during a class, the door opened and what should I see but Perkins' beaming face. I asked him to take a seat and wait until the end of the lesson.

The class had hardly ended when Perkins came up to me and amazed everyone with his animated conversation in Russian. He spoke freely but with many mistakes. However, except for me, no one noticed; and the students were dumb-founded by what seemed to them his shining knowledge of Russian.

The 22nd of July was set as the date for my thesis defense. Although I was assured that virtually no one fails this last stage, I was exceptionally anxious. This exam decided my future American career.

Varya agreed to go with me by car and this made the trip much easier. Even more, her presence distracted me from thinking about the outcome of this important exam. Everything went smoothly, without any messed-up questions. All the professors were amicably disposed and, after two hours, I was led out of the sanctuary where my fate was to be decided. My adviser and friend, Professor Menu, was the first to reappear, and he congratulated me on having received my doctor's degree. My joy was boundless.

After him, the other professors came out, congratulating me and wishing me success in my teaching career. They gave me several copies of my dissertation; and I took a taxi and went to a lawyer friend, Timinsky, to share my happiness and to phone Iowa. I knew that Yuri would be just as happy as I at such a successful conclusion of my three years of labor. My call woke Yuri up, even though it was already twelve o'clock there. He had been in a chess tournament in Chicago the night before and had returned very late. On hearing the good news he started to ask me all the details of the exam.

There is a Russian saying that joy shared with someone who genuinely sympathizes with you is double joy. After the conversation with Yuri, my spirits rose even further and, after visiting a few friends, Varya and I returned to New York.

The last two weeks of teaching in Columbia flew past very nicely and almost unnoticed. Almost everyone, the teachers as well as the students, tried to take note of my success and vied with each other in inviting me to celebrate. Of course, for me the defense of my dissertation and getting the Ph.D. was a very important event; now I knew my position in America was stable.

I decided to spend everything I had made at Columbia and go to Europe. The main purpose of this trip was to inform Marcel Aimé personally that my dissertation about him had enabled me to attain that position I had only been able to dream about in the past.

I did not think long about it; I bought the ticket and flew to Europe the first part of August. The first stage was Bad Kissengen and the Sanatarium Dietz, where I had been twice before. The consequences of starvation, the Leningrad blockade, and camp life in Germany were making themselves felt.

Upon my arrival in Bad Kissingen, I immediately phoned Marcel Aimé and this time asked for him personally. Then I phoned Tanya and invited her to spend some time with me.

Marcel Aimé was apparently very pleased with my success. He had earlier written me that he was sure that I would get the laurel wreath. Now he was sharing my joy and advised me to publish my dissertation in book form right away. I followed his advice and the book was published at the beginning of the next year by one of the large Parisian publishing houses, Mercure de France.

Soon Tanya arrived and spent a week with me, enjoying the pleasant pastimes in this charming German spa. I was also awaiting Dima who was in Europe at that time. Dima brought a charming young girl with him, Karin, the wife of his friend, Dr. Mosler. He had become acquainted with Dr. Mosler during his studies at Mainz, and now they were good friends. I liked Karin right away. With them was the Moslers' small son.

Dima was leading the boy around, all his attention given to seeing that no bees or other insects bit the child.

Since that time a wonderful relationship has existed between Karin and me, this despite the great difference in age. Many times afterward, I would visit these friendly people in Wurzburg where I would always feel at home.

This time I spent only a month in Europe and returned directly from Frankfurt to New York where I was met by Yuri and his friend Kolya. We went by car to Syracuse, spending one night at Kolya's parents. The next day Yuri and I continued our trip to Iowa.

Again I had to look for a place to live, since I had given up the apartment Françoise and I had the previous spring. I had to take what remained after the flood of students had picked them over. What I found was not very good. It was one room with a tiny kitchen in which it was difficult for even one person to turn around. The bathroom was shared with the neighbor, an elderly woman.

My colleagues were horrified on seeing this apartment. In comparison with the communal apartments in Russia or with the barracks in Germany, it did not seem so bad to me. It was a good thing that I had not been spoiled and was satisfied with things that others regarded as absolutely unacceptable. I did not share my American friends' opinion.

Some disappointment awaited me in the department. During my absence, there had been some changes. I had been put in a small separate office in which, to my great disappointment, there was no window. This was quite unpleasant because I just could not bear the overheating of most public buildings in America. Since I love fresh air, I had always had the habit of airing out the place. Here, however, because of the absence of any windows, it was impossible to do this. The heat and stuffiness were unbearable. I would come in a coat when it was cool on the street, but I would take it off immediately and remain in just a summer dress. This steambath, without windows, made my existence miserable.

There were many meetings of the Russian circle and I would often go to the movies with Dean Mills, a nice new student from Mt. Pleasant. Unfortunately, my French girls were gone. Both had returned to Paris, and I was living alone. Yuri came every day to eat dinner with me. A frequent visitor of mine was Miriam Gelfand. She and her husband, Larry, a professor of history, had moved to Iowa from Wyoming.

With Miriam, who had begun teaching in the Russian department, I immediately established a close friendship. She had a wonderful character, always ready to help. When I somehow twisted my back (I was always busy putting my "chic" apartment in order), only Miriam was helpful, taking me to the doctor and shopping for me. I appreciated her attitude and still appreciate it. Fortunately for me, the Gelfands settled in Iowa for good, which is rather infrequent in a university town. It is so nice to have friends for many years. Here in America, people are always moving somewhere when they can find better working conditions and more money.

In Russia there was a completely different relationship to money, apparently because nobody had any. We lived thus: you received your pay and you would be lucky if it lasted until the end of the month and you didn't have to borrow. And about savings, no one could even think about that. Wages and salaries went by specialty and were the same everywhere. No one tried to leave his nest.

Despite the wretchedness of my dwelling, I nonetheless, according to my custom, would put on Russian dinners and invite my acquaintances from the university. Unfortunately, however, it was on a very modest scale.

Yuri was playing chess often and had already gained quite a reputation, winning the Mid-West tournament. His studies at the university were also going very well, something that pleased me immensely. In Syracuse the main distraction from his studies were the girls to whom he was not at all indifferent. Being good-looking and having a friendly, cheerful nature, he had great success on campus and the girls were running after him. Here, for the time being, he was devoting more attention to his studies, to the displeasure of quite a number of the girls. They thought he was the most attractive fellow on our campus, something of which I was very proud but was afraid that such glory could hurt his studies.

At the beginning of February, 1963, Yuri asked my persmission to bring his girlfriend to supper. This was a girl about whom I had not yet even heard. She was quite a nice girl, but since she had already been married and was a number of years older than Yuri, I was quite uneasy. She gave an impression of someone who knew what she wanted and what her goals were. In this case, apparently, she wanted Yuri, who was gentle and pliable.

Uneasy over this, I shared my worries with Miriam. Naturally, I could not discuss such questions with my other student-friends.

My favorite Perkins, for example, thought it wonderful that his friend was also involved in a romantic affair. He encouraged Yuri in every way.

In March I was very happy over the publication, by Mercure de France in Paris, of my book, taken from my reworked dissertation. Marcel Aimé had kept his word. Françoise had also put in quite a bit of effort with the editing of this book.

In April I was invited to give a lecture at the University of Minnesota. I went there by car. I was giving a lecture in Russian and it seemed to me that few of those present understood it, this despite the fact that these were teachers of Russian language and/or literature. Then I noticed that one young man in the audience was listening attentively and correctly reacting to the content of the lecture.

After the conference, I became acquainted with him and told him my impression, that it seemed that he alone, of those professors present, understood what I was talking about. That day he invited me to give a lecture in the fall in Urbana, Illinois, where he was in charge of the Russian section of the conference. This young man was Norman Luxenburg.

Spring was approaching and with it the pull toward Europe. Yuri and Nancy (that was his girlfriend's name) had decided to spend two months together, at first at Menton in France where he had to attend a chemistry convention. They then wanted to go either to Spain or to Greece, where Nancy had already been and where she wanted to revisit. I wanted them to go to Spain because my cousin Pavel, who lived in Morocco, had offered to take us on a trip in his car. Of course, the young people were not especially interested in a trip under the observation of a mother and an uncle.

Nancy divorced her husband the 1st of May. I do not know the main reason for this decision, whether it was the relationship that had already existed between the couple or whether it was the appearance of Yuri. The affair was getting more involved and the light-hearted flirtation had been transformed into a serious romance. My heart was aching. I had hoped for something special for my beloved, good-looking, and capable son.

Everything about this nice-looking Nancy frightened me: her age, her self-assurance, her just-finalized divorce, the presence in Iowa City of her divorced husband, and, mainly, her persuading Yuri to tranfer to M.I.T. I again foresaw a separation from my son and loneliness.

Dima lived far away. Upon his return from Germany, where he had finished his studies with outstanding success and received the title of Doctor of medicine, he moved to Connecticut. During his stay in Germany, his wife had taken up philosophy and became acquainted with a philosopher whom she was now preparing to marry after a divorce from Dima.

At the beginning of June, Yuri, Pavel Batinic, and I left Iowa by car for New York. Nancy had left earlier with her brother, having made arrangements to meet Yuri a few days later and go to Amsterdam.

At the beginning of May of that year, 1963, I bought a house. What especially attracted me about this house was that there were three apartments in it, one for myself, one that I intended for Yuri, and the other to rent to my students in order that they would have more practice with the Russian language, something which is especially important in the study of foreign languages. On the 12th of May, Yuri and I put on a huge reception in the new house, to celebrate both the purchase of the house and my recently issued book. Except for a sofa, we had no furniture; however, this did not disturb us. We rented everything: tables, chairs, and dishes.

We invited some sixty persons. Everybody was there—many professors whom we knew: Vice-President Weaver with his wife; Yuri's friends and colleagues from the chemistry department; and all my medical doctors, headed by my surgeon Dr. Geiss, to whom I had been immensely grateful for the successful operation during my first few months in Iowa.

I prepared many hors d'oevres with the help of my assistant, Tamara; Yuri made a wonderful punch, pouring an especially large amount of cognac into it, thanks to which it was especially tasty but extremely strong. Many of the guests, expecting a harmless drink normally served at such receptions, were mistaken and became victims of this punch. Thus, one of Yuri's friends was unable to leave our house and spent the night there. In the morning, embarrassed, he tried to leave before I showed up.

This year that had begun so well turned out to be the most tragic year of my life. The bombs, the hunger, war, the camp, all of those experiences paled before the horrible event which took place the 26th of July, 1963. Yuri and Nancy died during the earthquake in Skopje, Yugoslavia. They had stopped to spend one night on their way to Greece, where Nancy had insisted on going after their stay in France.

At that time I was again in Bad Kissingen where I was taking treatment. The summer had been especially happy and pleasant. It had seemed as though truly all the difficulties were behind us: the doctorate had been received; the situation in the university definitely secure; the book had been published; the house had been bought. What else would one hope for?

In June, with my niece Tanya, I had gone to Rimini, Italy where I had taken a large room with a private bath and all conveniences. It was unbelievably inexpensive, $10 a night, including all meals for two! We remained there until the 5th of July, enjoying the wonderful weather and the sea.

Then I went to my beloved Bad Kissingen where I became reacquainted with all the clients and was having a wonderful time. There was much there to entertain a person. We went mushroom-hunting in the forest and on rides. A wealthy, elderly German made me very happy. Every day he would order a horse and carriage for several hours. He would seat himself in the carriage with several ladies from the sanatorium, while I picked the place on the coachbox and drove the horses as I used to do in my childhood on Father's estate.

From Yuri's letters I knew that instead of the intended trip to Spain, the young people were going to Greece and were preparing to take this long trip by motorcycle. On July 26th I was listening to the news as usual. They were showing the earthquake in Skopje which had taken place at five o'clock that morning. I felt a pressure on my heart and a sudden premonition. There was no logical reason for this premonition. Why should I have supposed that just on that particular day Nancy and Yuri would be in Skopje? The trip from France to Greece was long. I had no idea whatsoever where they were, especially since Yuri wrote me very seldom. One could have supposed that they were still in France or even already in Greece.

However, the feeling of something awful approaching me, did not leave.

On the morning of July 28 there was a phone call from Paris. Tanya's husband was phoning and informing me that according to information received by French journalists, a motorcycle with french registration in the name of Garder (Tanya's husband's name) had been found in Skopje. I knew instantly that this was the motorcycle Yuri had bought in Paris and had registered under the name of Garder. I could not utter a word and dropped the receiver.

Later the doctor, making his morning rounds, found me in a incoherent state. I was crying, screaming, and kept repeating one word "why?" The doctor himself, only one month before that, had lost his only son in an auto accident. He said to me, "I also kept asking that one question, 'why?' "

The following days cannot be described. For the first time in my life I was completely lost and did not know what to do, where to go, where and from whom to seek aid. The main thing was to find out whether Yuri was alive, for the hope still persisted that he had not perished but, perhaps, was lying somewhere in a hospital. Indeed, nothing had been heard officially. I went to the Russian church, to our beloved priest. He liked Yuri very much, as did his old wife. Learning what had occurred, he said several prayers for me for Yuri's health and safe return.

The next day, acquaintances took me to the American embassy in Frankfurt. An American woman, who had an important position in the embassy, personally tried to help. She got connected with Skopje, but the news was not very reassuring. In the ruined Hotel Macedonia, amidst the rubble on the first floor, they had found the passports of both Nancy and Yuri. The American woman embraced me and told me this painful news.

It seemed to me that with each word of hers, life was flowing out of me. There were no tears, only a torturing, almost physical pain in my heart. It seemed that all light had gone out and that the creature in the embrace of this stranger was not I, but someone else.

What came later? The return to the sanatorium, the sympathy and aid of strangers, phone calls from various friends who had heard about my tragedy. From America, besides the innumerable telegrams, was a note from Dima that he was flying to join me. I received all this as though it were something alien, not concerning me directly. I would fall asleep only after having heavy dosages of sedatives.

Dima arrived as did the Moslers. Visas were obtained and tickets, too. Dima and I decided to go to Skopje. For the first several days, access had been forbidden because of repeated tremors. Dima rented a car and we drove to Frankfurt. From there we went by train to Yugoslavia. All that night I sat by the window in our first-class compartment, going over everything I had lived through, all the harsh blows of fate. All of them seemed like nothing in comparison with this sorrow. Fate seemed implacable to me, fate that had so cruelly taken away the life of this young boy, full of hope and strength this young boy who had already gone through so much in his short life and who finally had achieved what he was striving for.

This death seemed so senseless to me now that the bombing and the starvation of the war had become only memories. Yuri had become an American, an equal citizen of the new society, of the new country where all paths were open for a better future. Then, suddenly, death had come in a place where he had spent only one night! In no way could I reconcile myself with this!

We spent a day amidst the ruins of Skopje. A German Red Cross team, headed by a doctor, were trying their utmost to help. But what could they do?

The excavation continued. We were taken to a large shed where the belongings of those who had died had been laid out. The heat was unbearable. I simply could not get myself to dig into this pile of things in the hopes of finding something that belonged to Yuri and thus, have one more confirmation of his death.

And yet, a small hope still remained. The kind Germans took us in their car to the American hospital, about twenty km from Skopje. They too were very nice to us, but we found no trace of Yuri. I was advised to give the address of the dentist who had cared for him in Iowa. That could help in the identification of the corpses.

A tall, American airforce captain came up to me after learning that I was from Iowa. He too had graduated from our university. "When we find your son, alive or dead, I will bring him to wherever you wish," he told me. This heartfelt sympathy was too much for me. Through my sobbing, I named Wiesbaden. On August 17, 1963 a small group of close relatives gathered at the Orthodox cemetery in Wiesbaden. There, what remained of Yuri was committed to the earth.

Now that I am writing these lines, almost twenty years have passed since that tragic event, but I still do not know how and why I survived this most agonizing and terrible time of my life.